Elephant Man

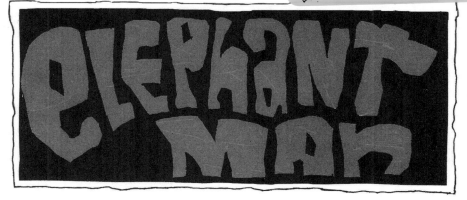

Also by Houston:
Vatican Hustle, $11.95

See more at our website:
www.nbmpublishing.com

P&H: $4 1st item, $1 each addt'l.

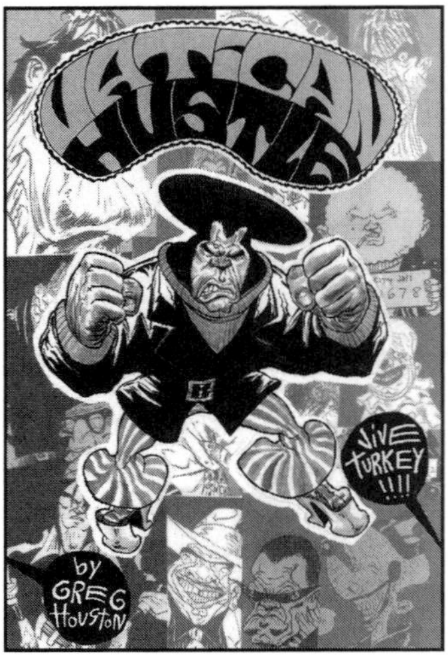
VATICAN HUSTLE
JIVE TURKEY !!!!
by GREG HOUSTON

We have over 200 titles,
write for our color catalog:
NBM
40 Exchange Pl., Ste. 1308
New York, NY. 10005

ISBN 978-1-56163-588-7

Library of Congress Control Number: 2010908354
1st printing, July 2010

by
GREG
HOUSTON

NANTIER · BEALL · MINOUSTCHINE
Publishing inc.
new york

Bio

Greg Houston was born in the great city of Baltimore in 1966. He graduated from Pratt Institute in 1988 and has been eking out a meager living as an illustrator ever since. He's won a few awards (including the 1998 Regional ADDY for Illustration and the 1972 Tony for Best Actor in a Musical for Pippin) and has worked for clients in nearly all facets of the illustration profession. He occasionally teaches illustration at Maryland Institute College of Art. On most days he can be found indulging in his twin passions of hobo fighting and ritualistic sacrifices. He enjoys blaxploitation films, women with lengthy prison sentences, and fire. He lives with his fiancee, loyal dog and two cats (one of which seems to distrust him).

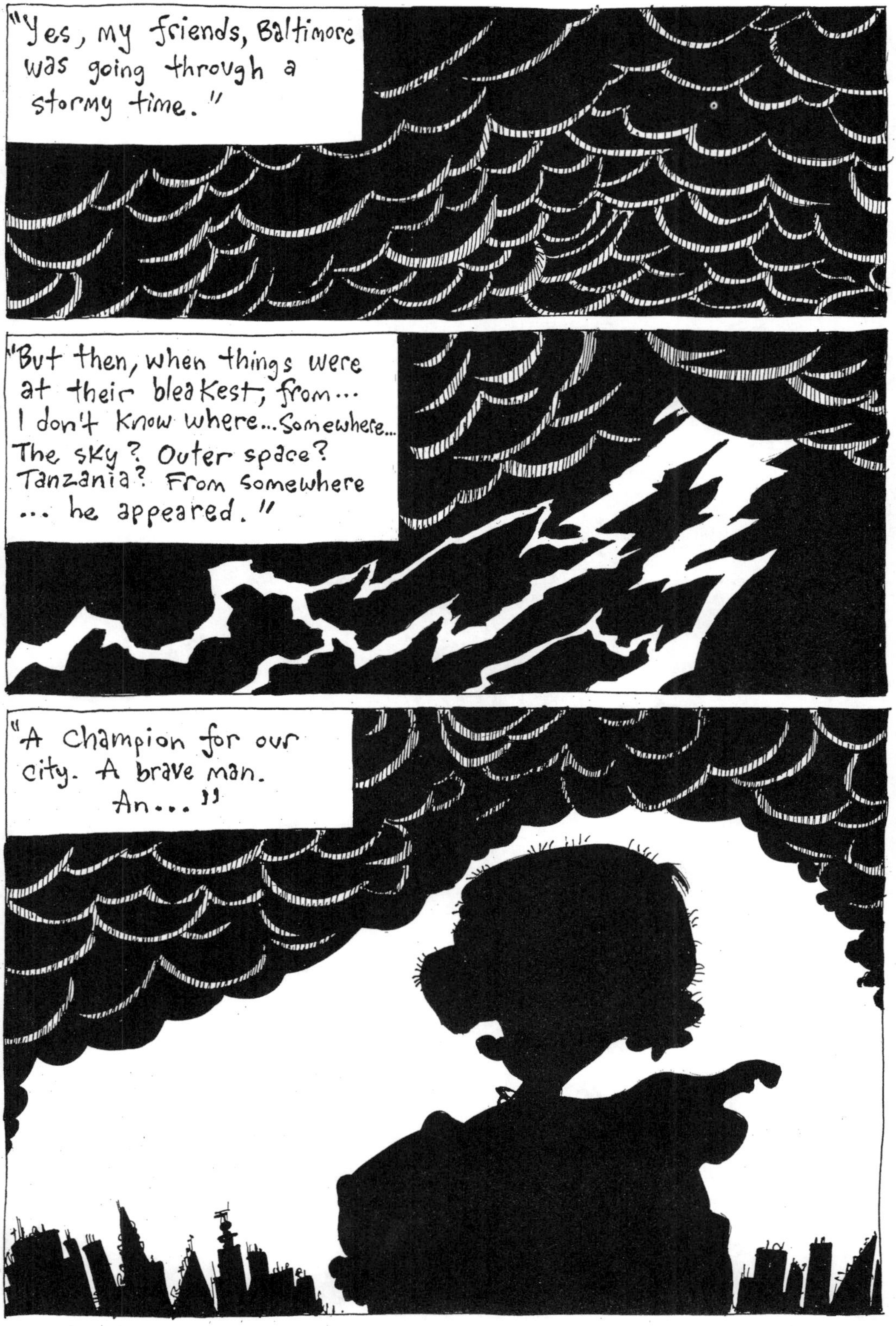
"Yes, my friends, Baltimore was going through a stormy time."
"But then, when things were at their bleakest, from... I don't know where... somewhere... The sky? Outer space? Tanzania? From somewhere ... he appeared."
"A Champion for our city. A brave man. An..."

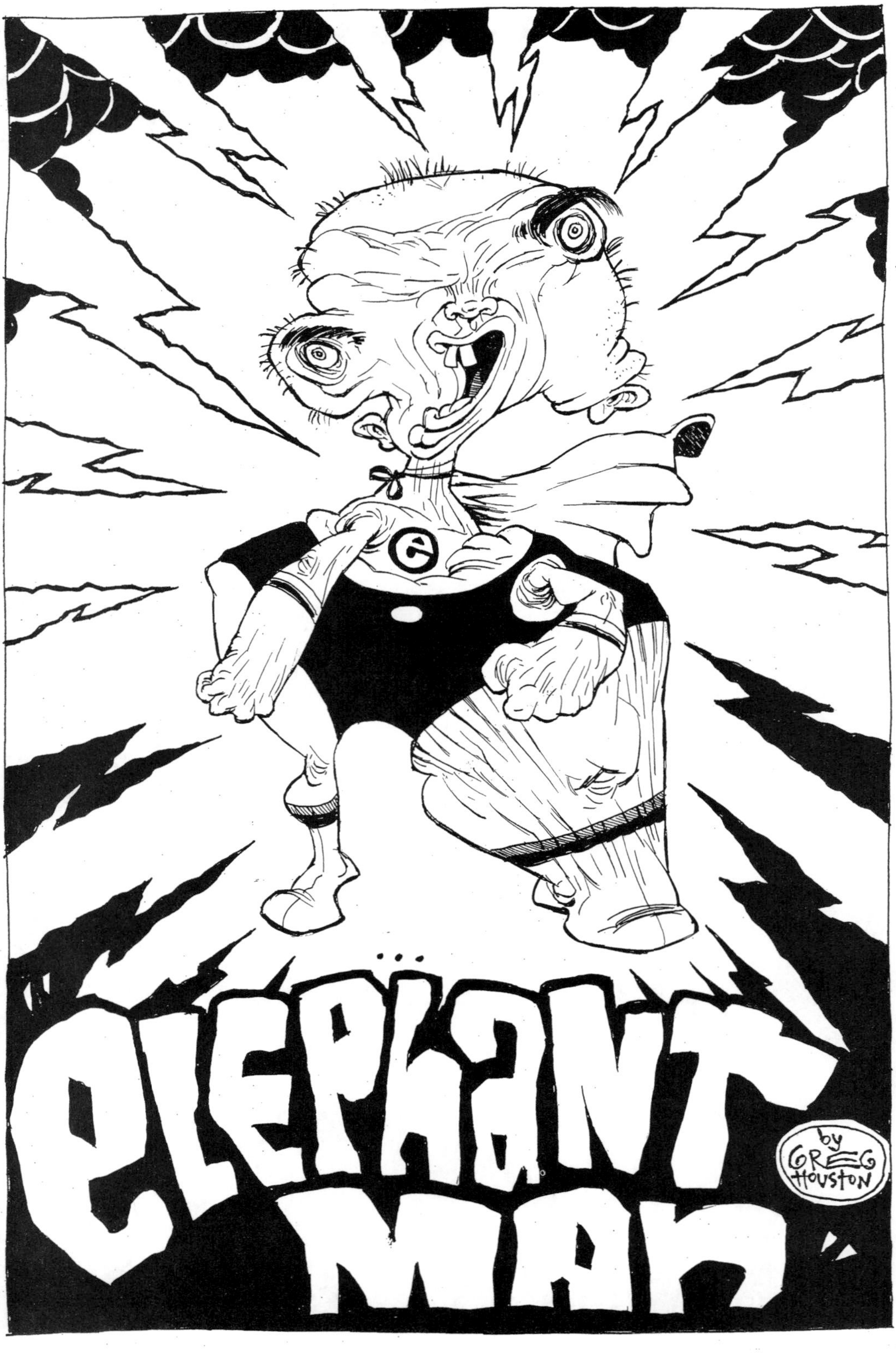
"Elephant Man"
by Greg Houston

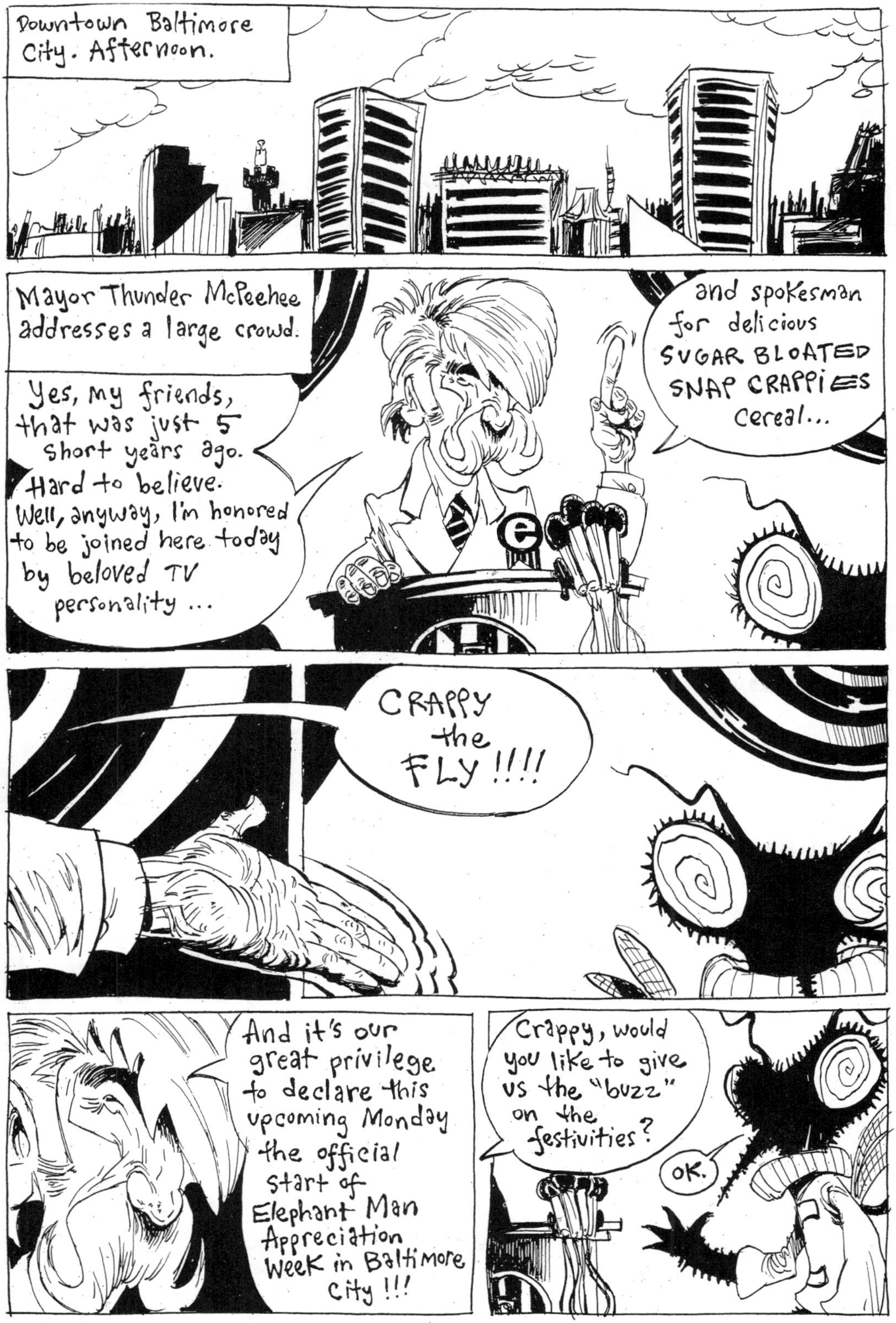

Downtown Baltimore City. Afternoon.
Mayor Thunder McPeehee addresses a large crowd.
Yes, my friends, that was just 5 short years ago. Hard to believe. Well, anyway, I'm honored to be joined here today by beloved TV personality ...
and spokesman for delicious SUGAR BLOATED SNAP CRAPPIES cereal...
CRAPPY the FLY !!!!
And it's our great privilege to declare this upcoming Monday the official start of Elephant Man Appreciation Week in Baltimore City !!!
Crappy, would you like to give us the "buzz" on the festivities?
OK.

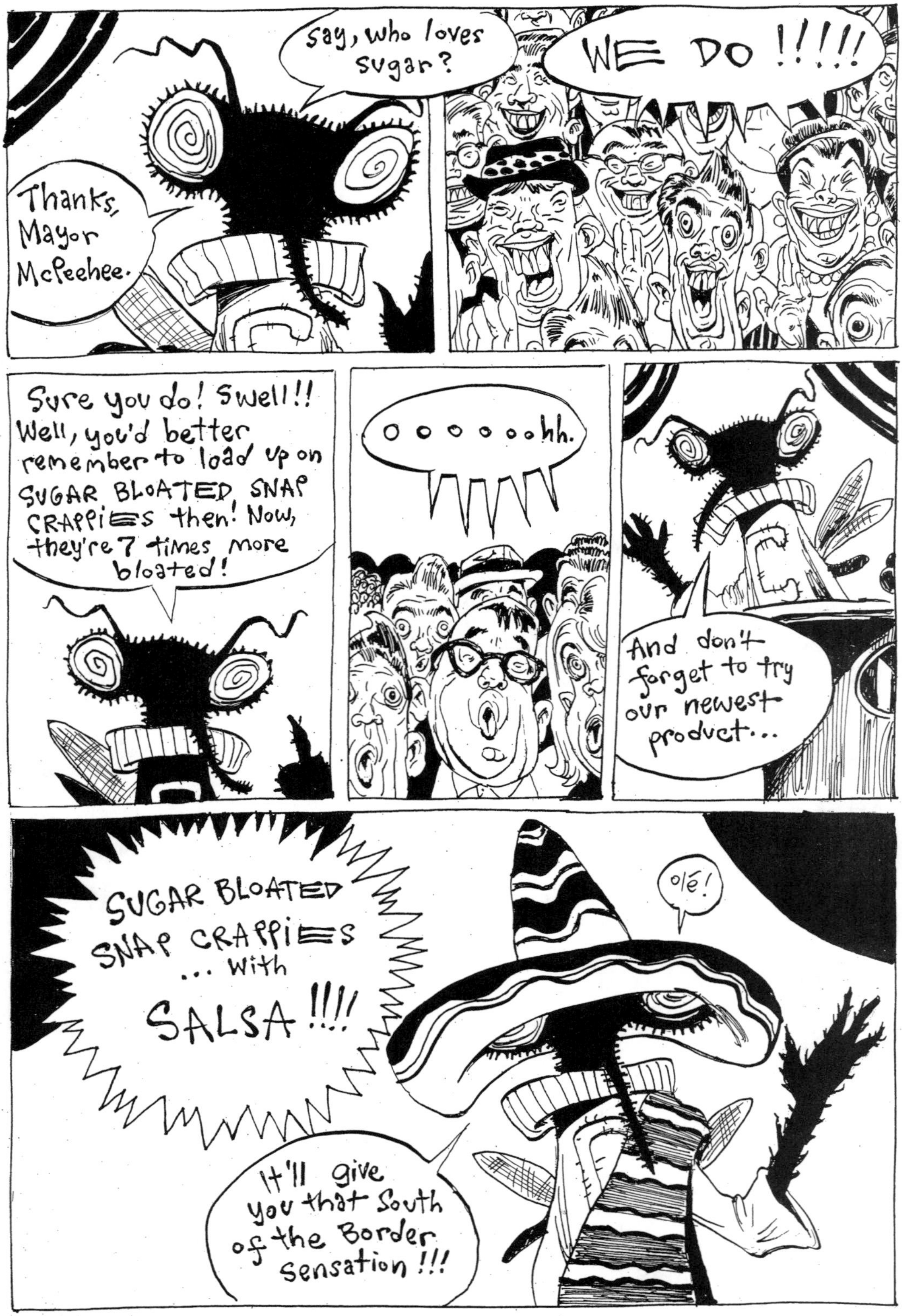
Thanks, Mayor McPeehee.
say, who loves sugar?
WE DO !!!!!
Sure you do! Swell!! Well, you'd better remember to load up on SUGAR BLOATED SNAP CRAPPIES then! Now, they're 7 times more bloated!
Oooooohh.
And don't forget to try our newest product...
SUGAR BLOATED SNAP CRAPPIES ... with SALSA!!!!
olé!
It'll give you that South of the Border sensation!!!

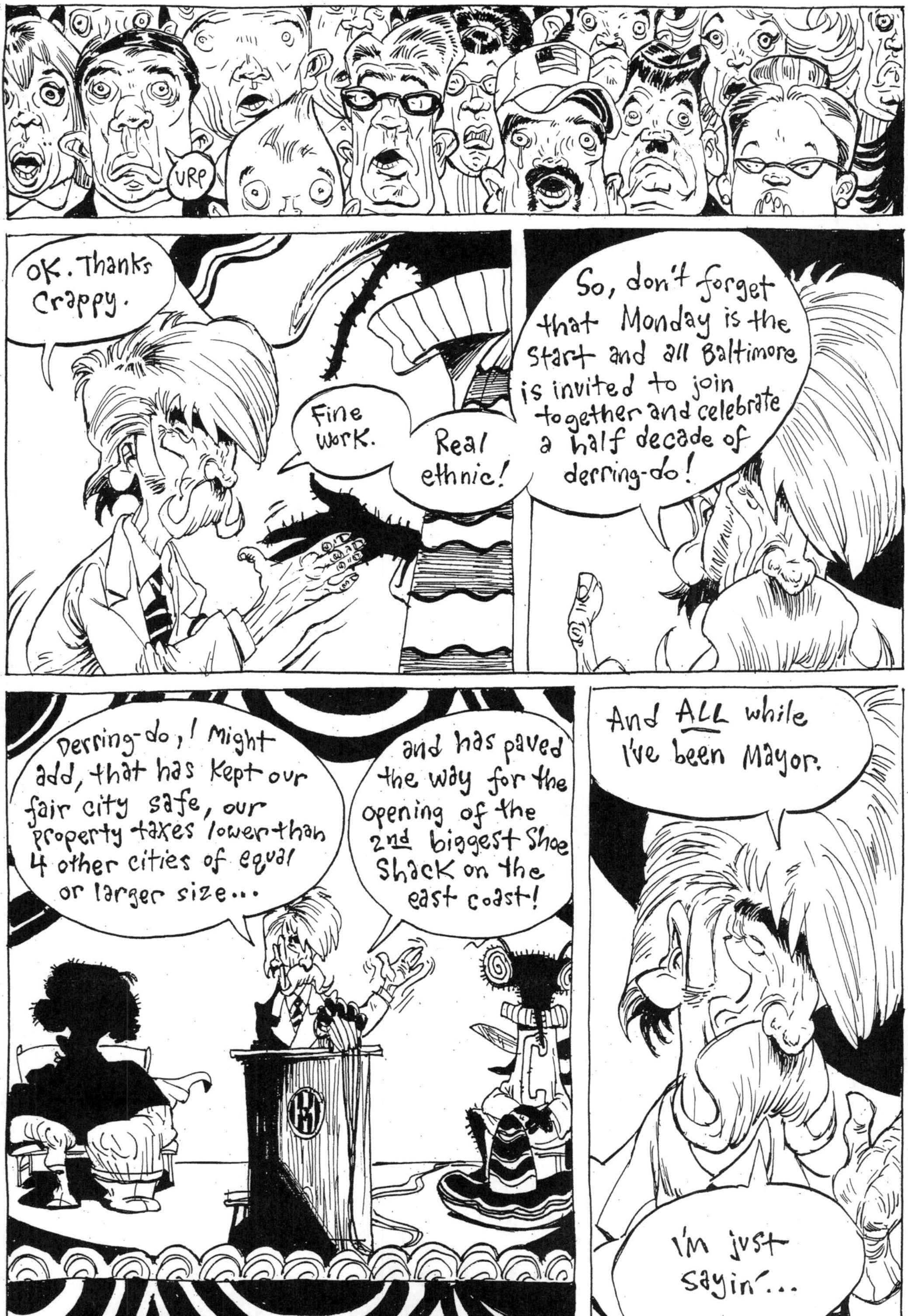
URP
OK. Thanks Crappy.
Fine work.
Real ethnic!
So, don't forget that Monday is the start and all Baltimore is invited to join together and celebrate a half decade of derring-do!
Derring-do, I might add, that has kept our fair city safe, our property taxes lower than 4 other cities of equal or larger size...
and has paved the way for the opening of the 2nd biggest Shoe Shack on the east coast!
And ALL while I've been Mayor.
I'm just sayin'...

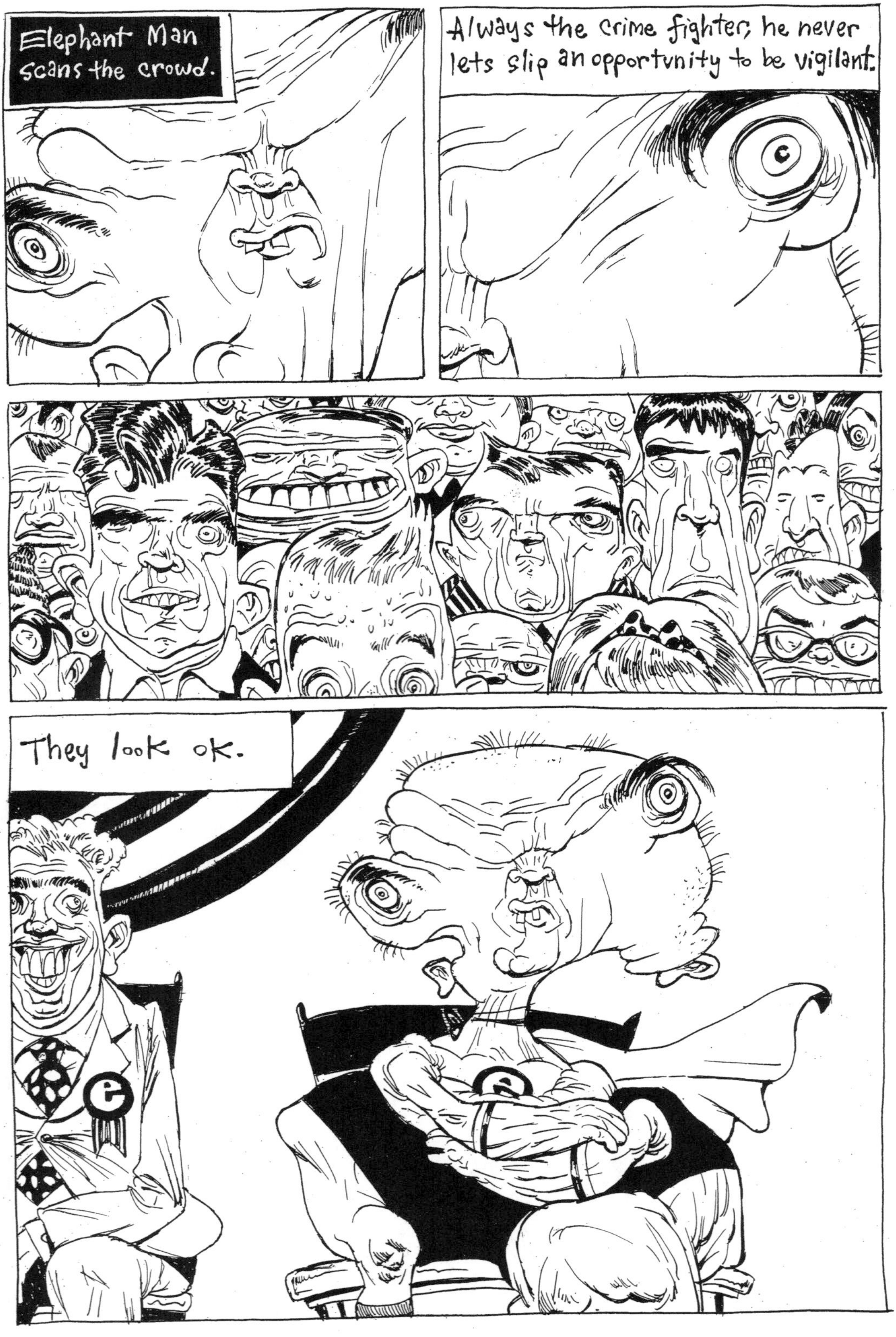
Elephant Man scans the crowd.
Always the crime fighter, he never lets slip an opportunity to be vigilant.
They look ok.

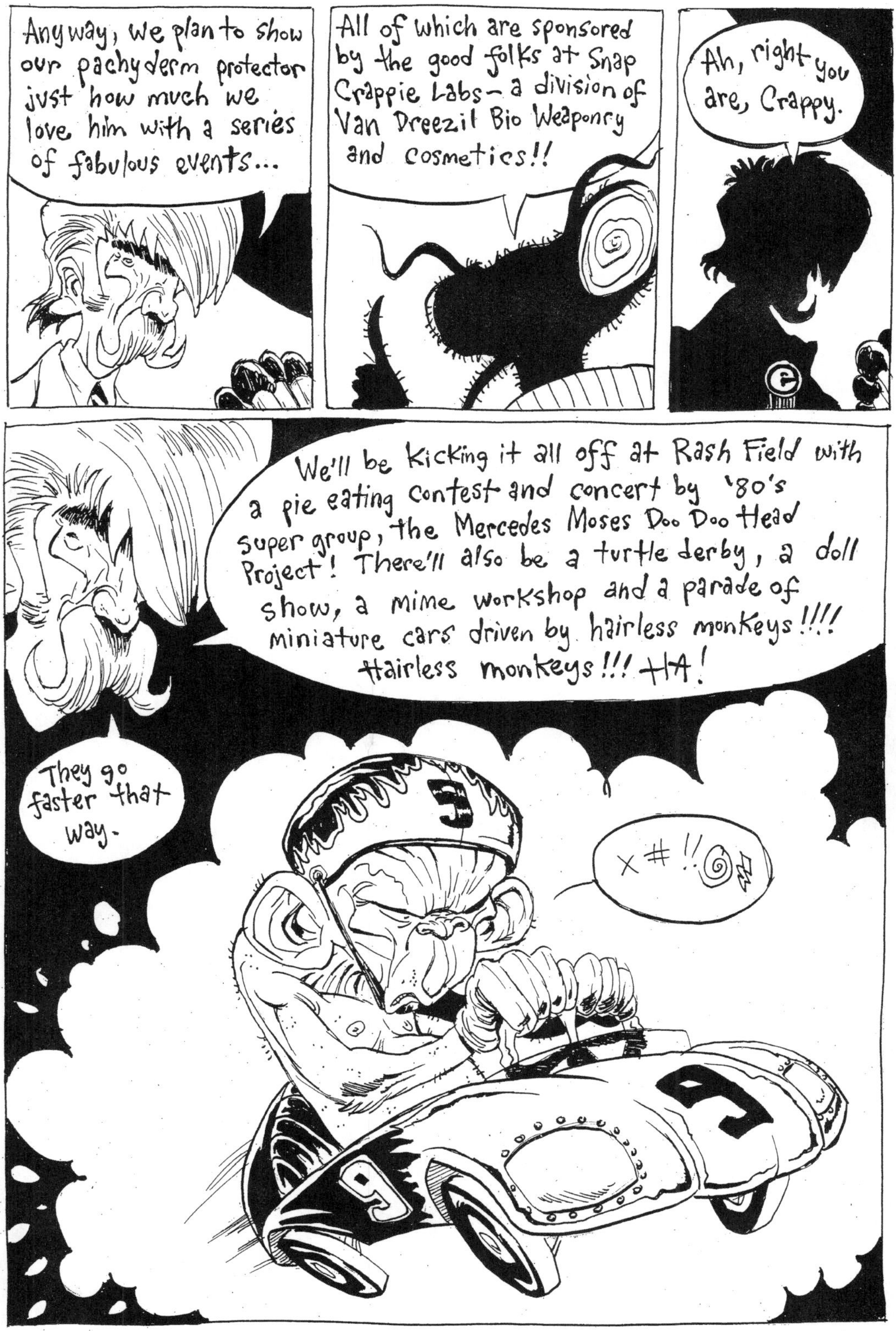
Anyway, we plan to show our pachyderm protector just how much we love him with a series of fabulous events...
All of which are sponsored by the good folks at Snap Crappie Labs— a division of Van Dreezil Bio Weaponry and cosmetics!!
Ah, right you are, Crappy.
We'll be kicking it all off at Rash Field with a pie eating contest and concert by '80's super group, the Mercedes Moses Doo Doo Head Project! There'll also be a turtle derby, a doll show, a mime workshop and a parade of miniature cars driven by hairless monkeys!!!! Hairless monkeys!!! HA!
They go faster that way.
x#!!

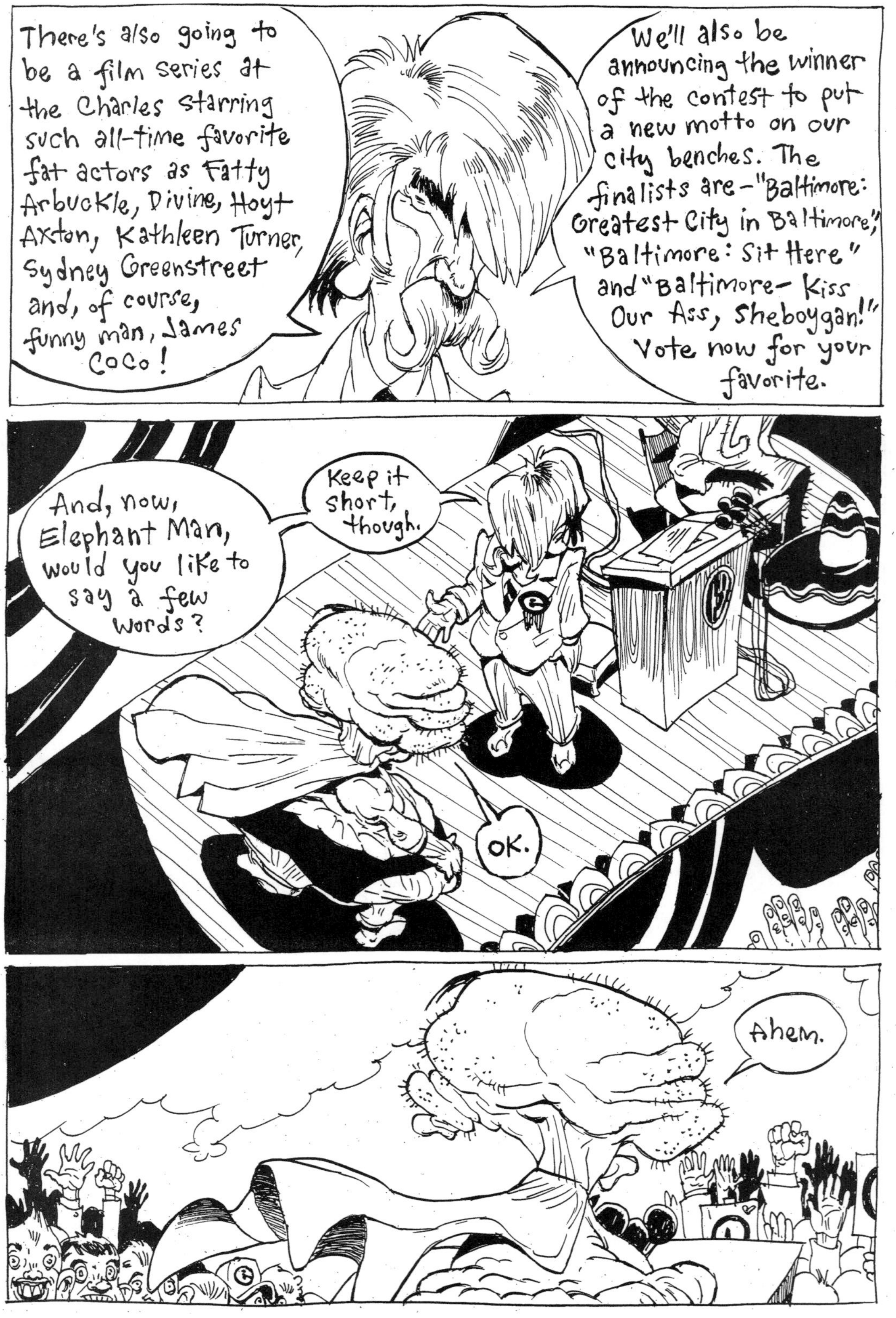
There's also going to be a film series at the Charles starring such all-time favorite fat actors as Fatty Arbuckle, Divine, Hoyt Axton, Kathleen Turner, Sydney Greenstreet and, of course, funny man, James CoCo!
We'll also be announcing the winner of the contest to put a new motto on our city benches. The finalists are – "Baltimore: Greatest City in Baltimore", "Baltimore: Sit Here" and "Baltimore– Kiss Our Ass, Sheboygan!" Vote now for your favorite.
And, now, Elephant Man, would you like to say a few words?
Keep it short, though.
OK.
Ahem.

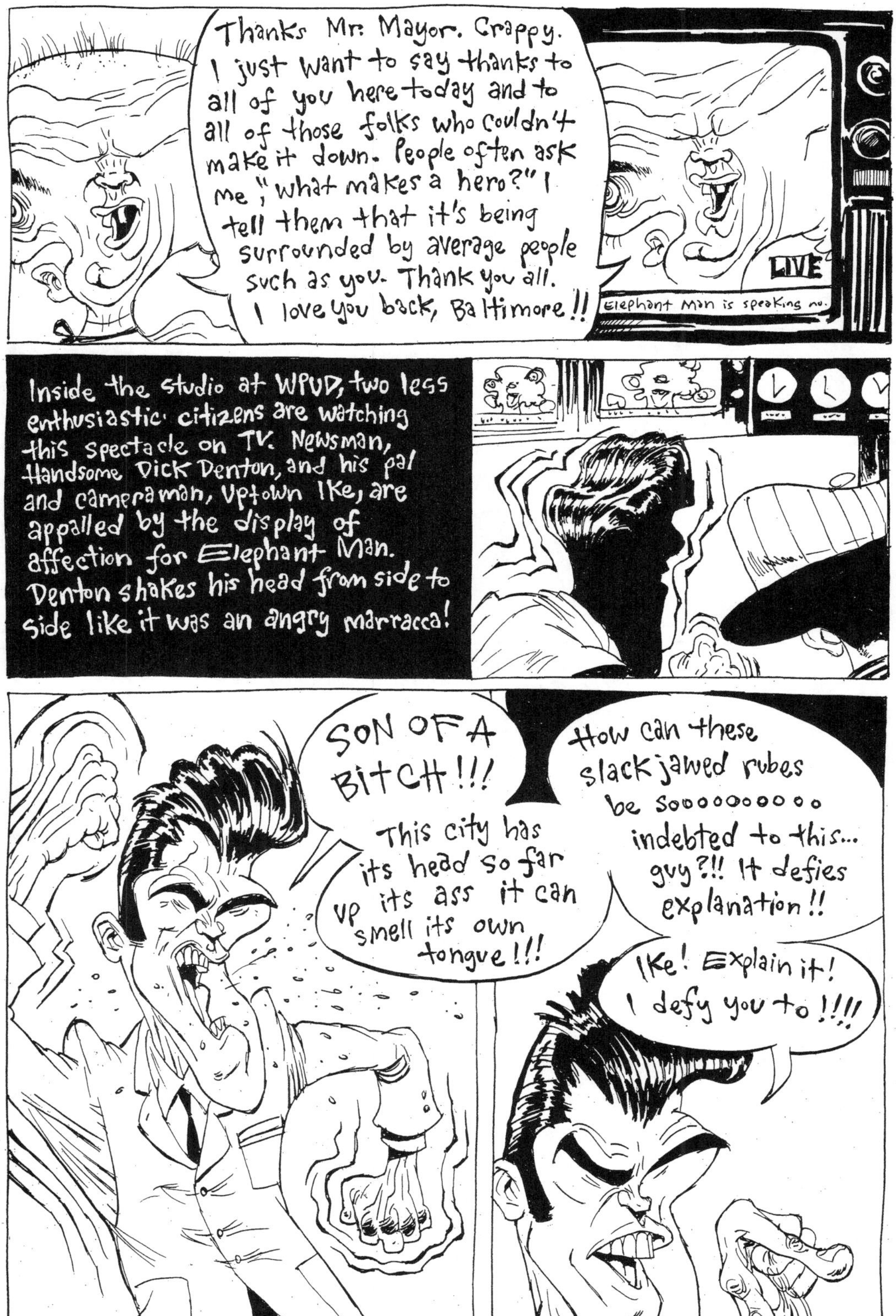
Thanks Mr. Mayor. Crappy. I just want to say thanks to all of you here today and to all of those folks who couldn't make it down. People often ask me, "what makes a hero?" I tell them that it's being surrounded by average people such as you. Thank you all. I love you back, Baltimore!!
LIVE
Elephant Man is speaking no.
Inside the studio at WPUD, two less enthusiastic citizens are watching this spectacle on TV. Newsman, Handsome Dick Denton, and his pal and cameraman, Uptown Ike, are appalled by the display of affection for Elephant Man. Denton shakes his head from side to side like it was an angry marracca!
SON OF A BITCH!!!
This city has its head so far up its ass it can smell its own tongue!!!
How can these slack jawed rubes be sooooooooo indebted to this... guy?!! It defies explanation!!
Ike! Explain it! I defy you to!!!!

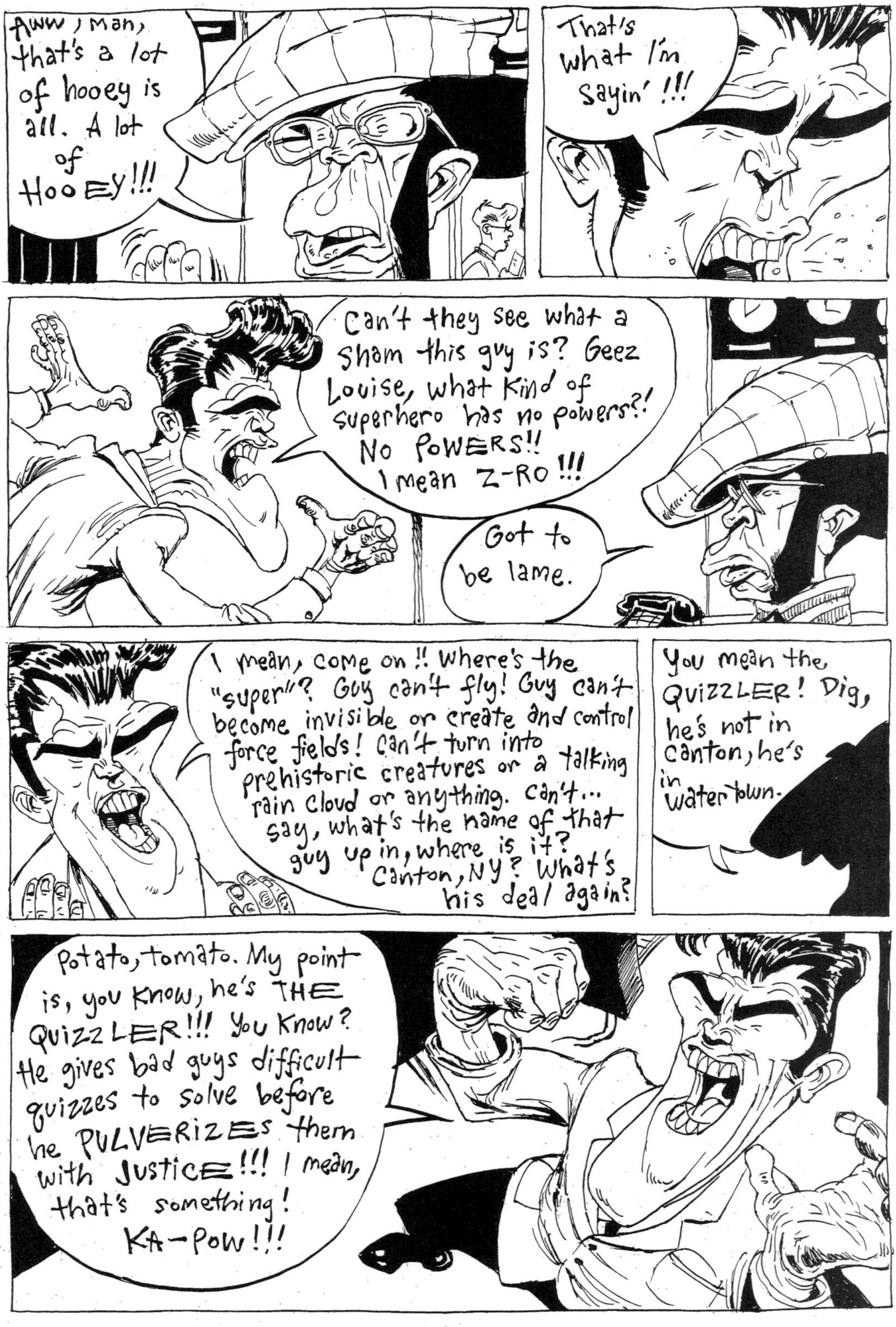
Aww, man, that's a lot of hooey is all. A lot of HOOEY!!!
That's what I'm sayin'!!!
Can't they see what a sham this guy is? Geez Louise, what kind of superhero has no powers?! No POWERS!! I mean Z-RO!!!
Got to be lame.
I mean, come on!! Where's the "super"? Guy can't fly! Guy can't become invisible or create and control force fields! Can't turn into prehistoric creatures or a talking rain cloud or anything. Can't... say, what's the name of that guy up in, where is it? Canton, NY? What's his deal again?
You mean the QUIZZLER! Dig, he's not in Canton, he's in Watertown.
Potato, tomato. My point is, you know, he's THE QUIZZLER!!! You know? He gives bad guys difficult quizzes to solve before he PULVERIZES them with JUSTICE!!! I mean, that's something! KA-POW!!!

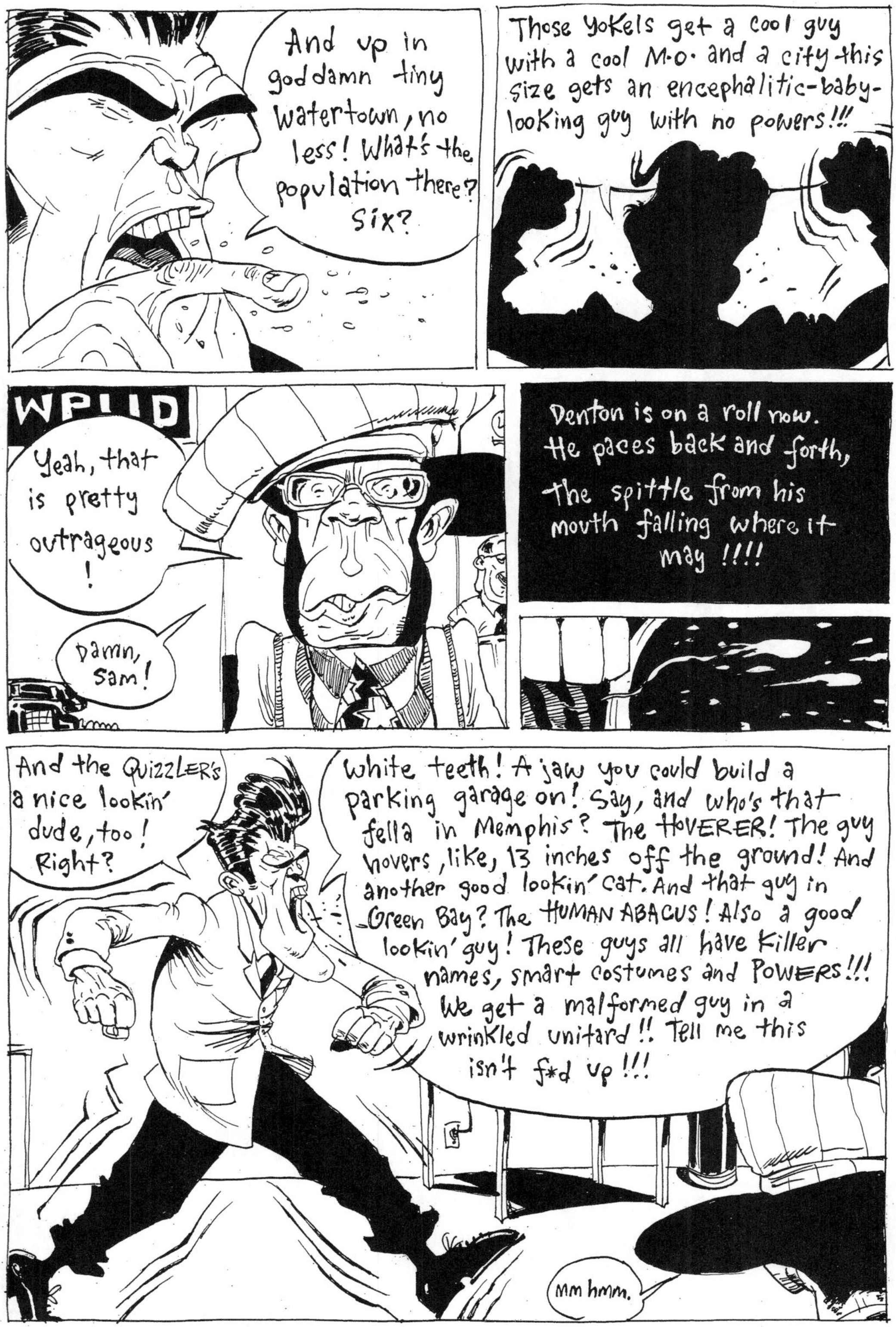
And up in goddamn tiny watertown, no less! What's the population there? Six?
Those yokels get a cool guy with a cool M.O. and a city this size gets an encephalitic-baby-looking guy with no powers!!!
WPUD
Yeah, that is pretty outrageous!
Damn, Sam!
Denton is on a roll now. He paces back and forth, the spittle from his mouth falling where it may!!!!
And the QUIZZLER's a nice lookin' dude, too! Right?
White teeth! A jaw you could build a parking garage on! Say, and who's that fella in Memphis? The HOVERER! The guy hovers, like, 13 inches off the ground! And another good lookin' cat. And that guy in Green Bay? The HUMAN ABACUS! Also a good lookin' guy! These guys all have killer names, smart costumes and POWERS!!! We get a malformed guy in a wrinkled unitard!! Tell me this isn't f*d up!!!
Mm hmm.

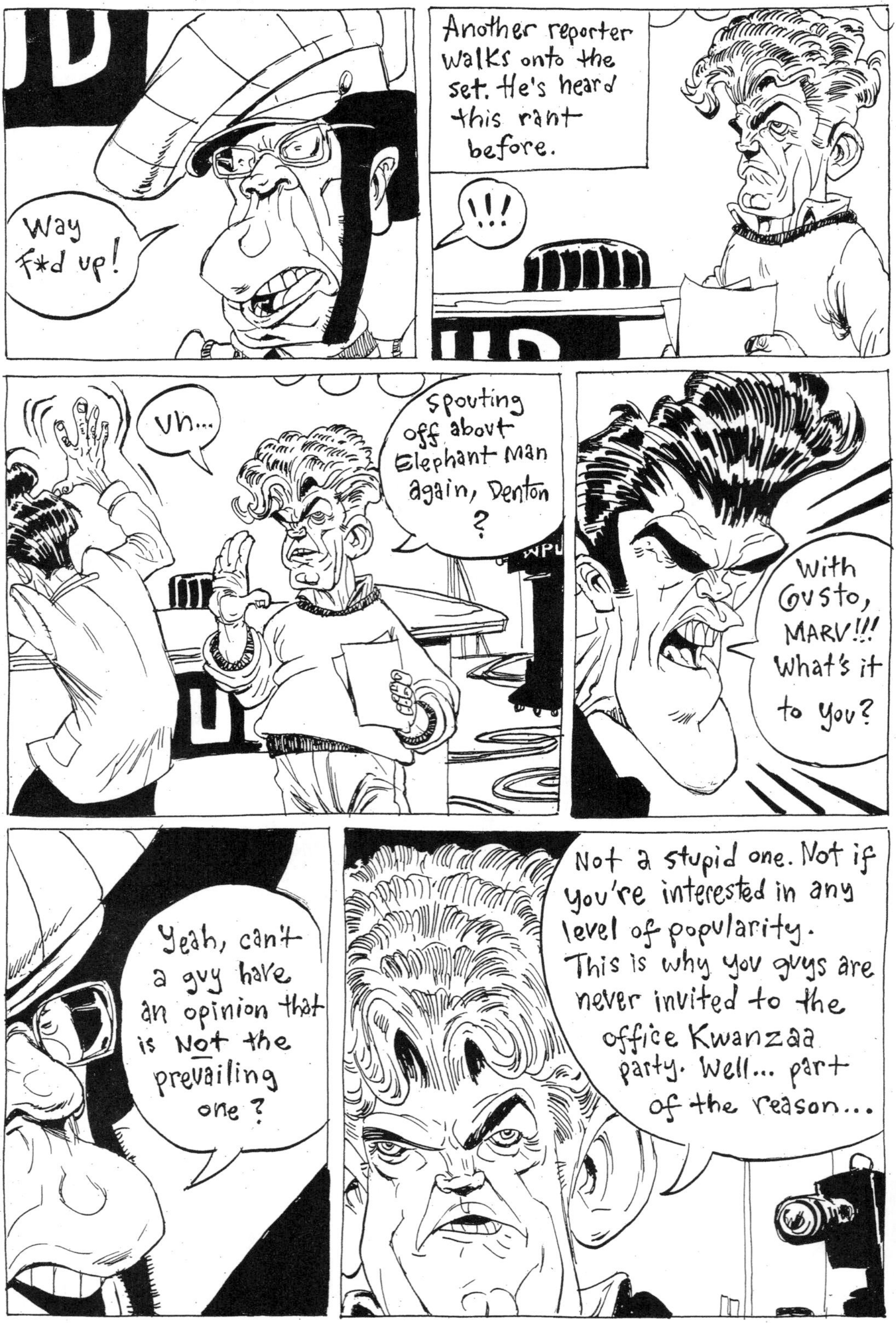
Way F*d up!
Another reporter walks onto the set. He's heard this rant before.
!!!
Uh...
Spouting off about Elephant Man again, Denton?
WPU
With Gusto, MARV!!! What's it to you?
Yeah, can't a guy have an opinion that is NOT the prevailing one?
Not a stupid one. Not if you're interested in any level of popularity. This is why you guys are never invited to the office Kwanzaa party. Well... part of the reason...

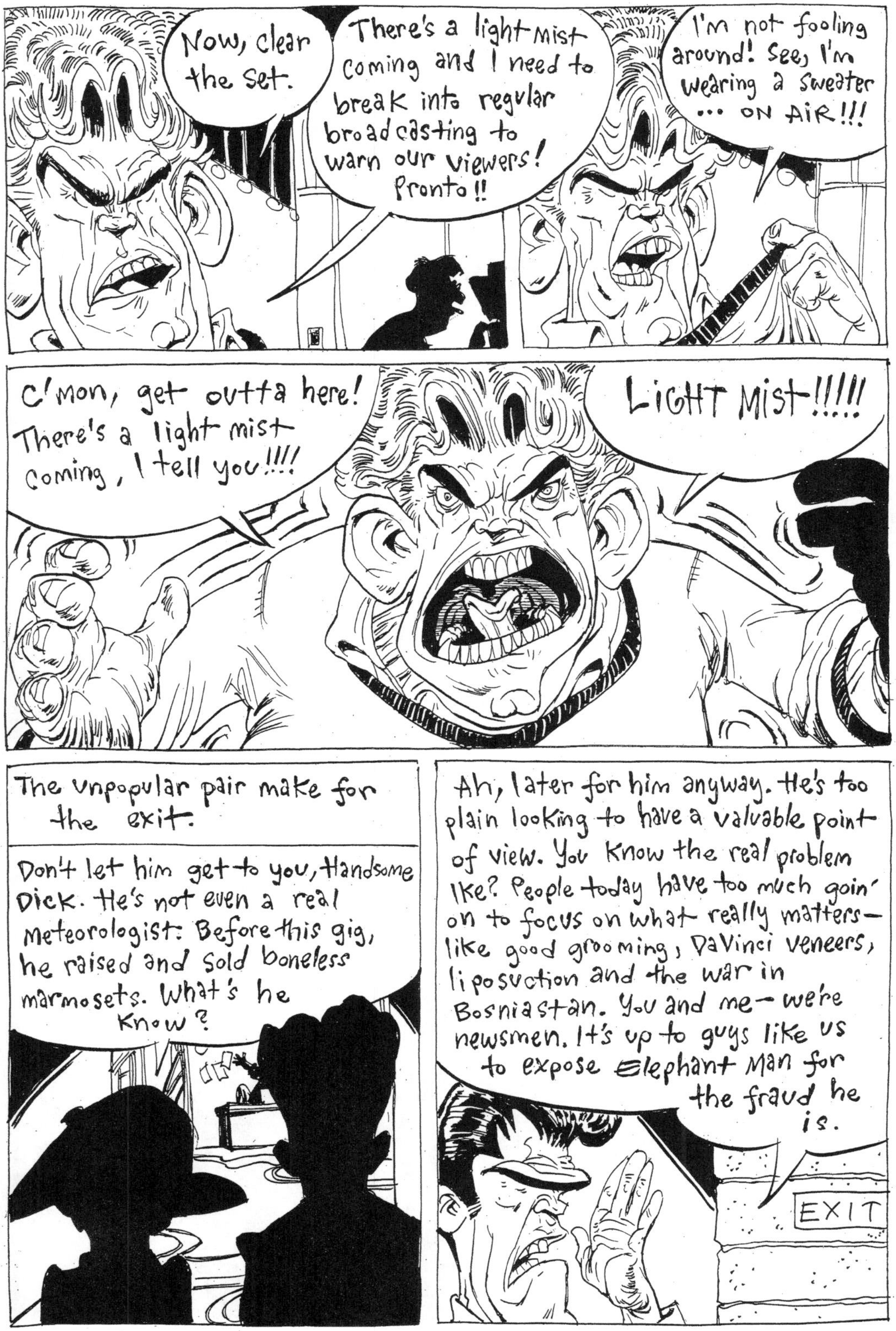
Now, clear the set.
There's a light mist coming and I need to break into regular broadcasting to warn our viewers! Pronto!!
I'm not fooling around! See, I'm wearing a sweater ... ON AIR!!!
C'mon, get outta here! There's a light mist coming, I tell you!!!!
LIGHT MIST!!!!!
The unpopular pair make for the exit.
Don't let him get to you, Handsome Dick. He's not even a real Meteorologist. Before this gig, he raised and sold boneless marmosets. What's he know?
Ah, later for him anyway. He's too plain looking to have a valuable point of view. You know the real problem Ike? People today have too much goin' on to focus on what really matters— like good grooming, DaVinci veneers, liposuction and the war in Bosniastan. You and me— we're newsmen. It's up to guys like us to expose Elephant Man for the fraud he is.
EXIT

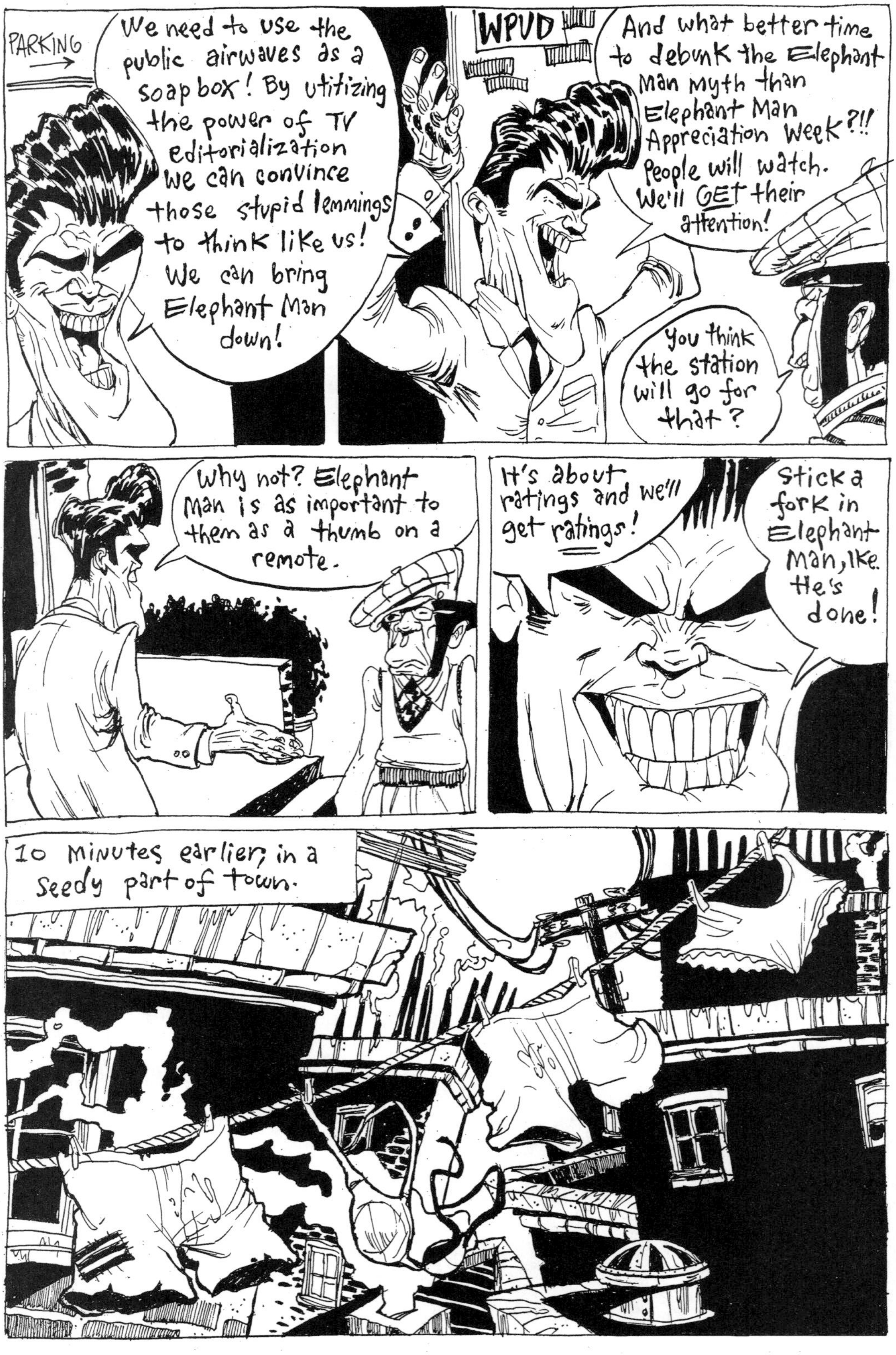
PARKING
We need to use the public airwaves as a soap box! By utitizing the power of TV editorialization we can convince those stupid lemmings to think like us! We can bring Elephant Man down!
WPUD
And what better time to debunk the Elephant Man myth than Elephant Man Appreciation Week?!! People will watch. We'll GET their attention!
You think the station will go for that?
Why not? Elephant Man is as important to them as a thumb on a remote.
It's about ratings and we'll get ratings!
Stick a fork in Elephant Man, Ike. He's done!
10 Minutes earlier, in a seedy part of town.

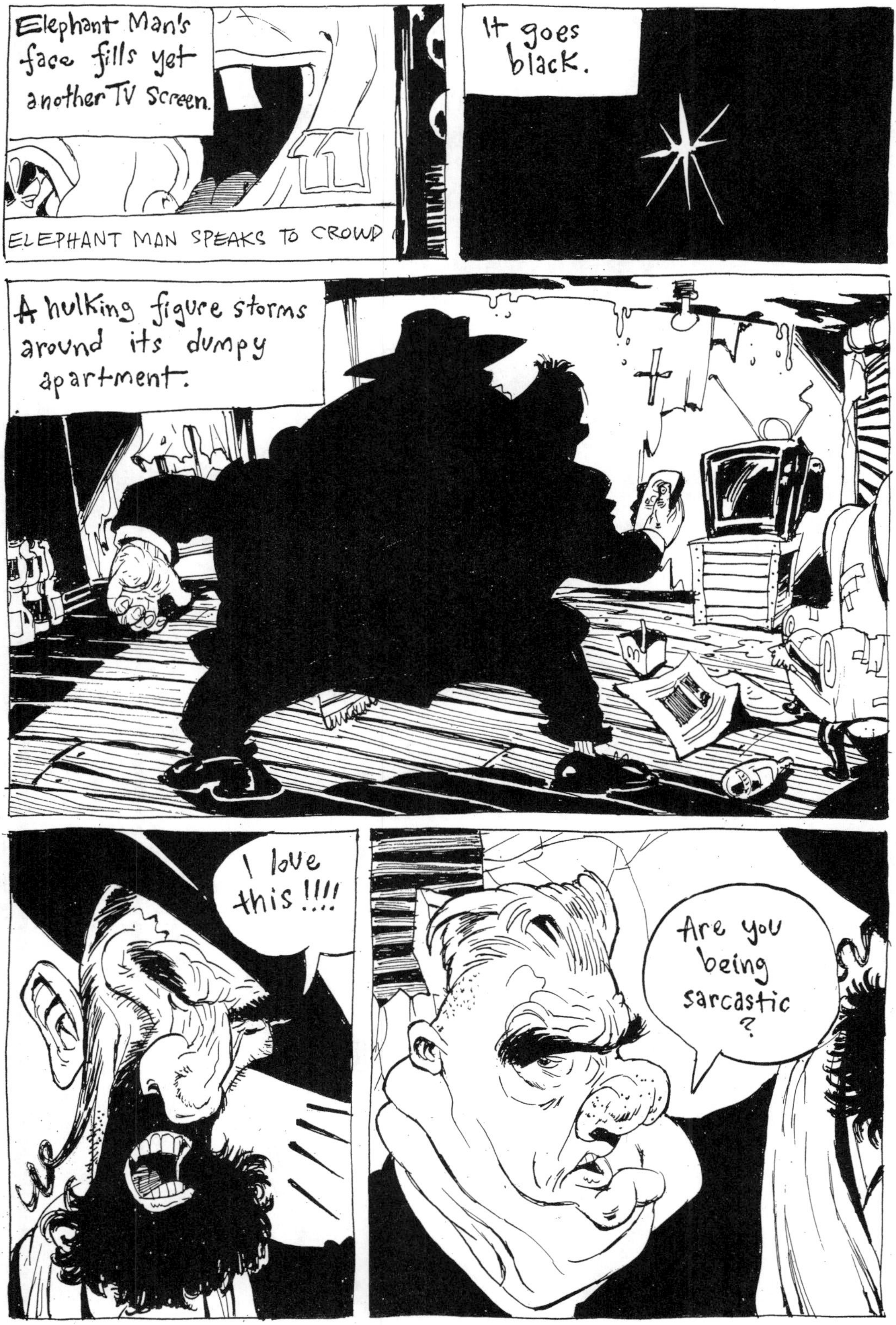
Elephant Man's face fills yet another TV screen.
ELEPHANT MAN SPEAKS TO CROWD
It goes black.
A hulking figure storms around its dumpy apartment.
I love this !!!!
Are you being sarcastic ?

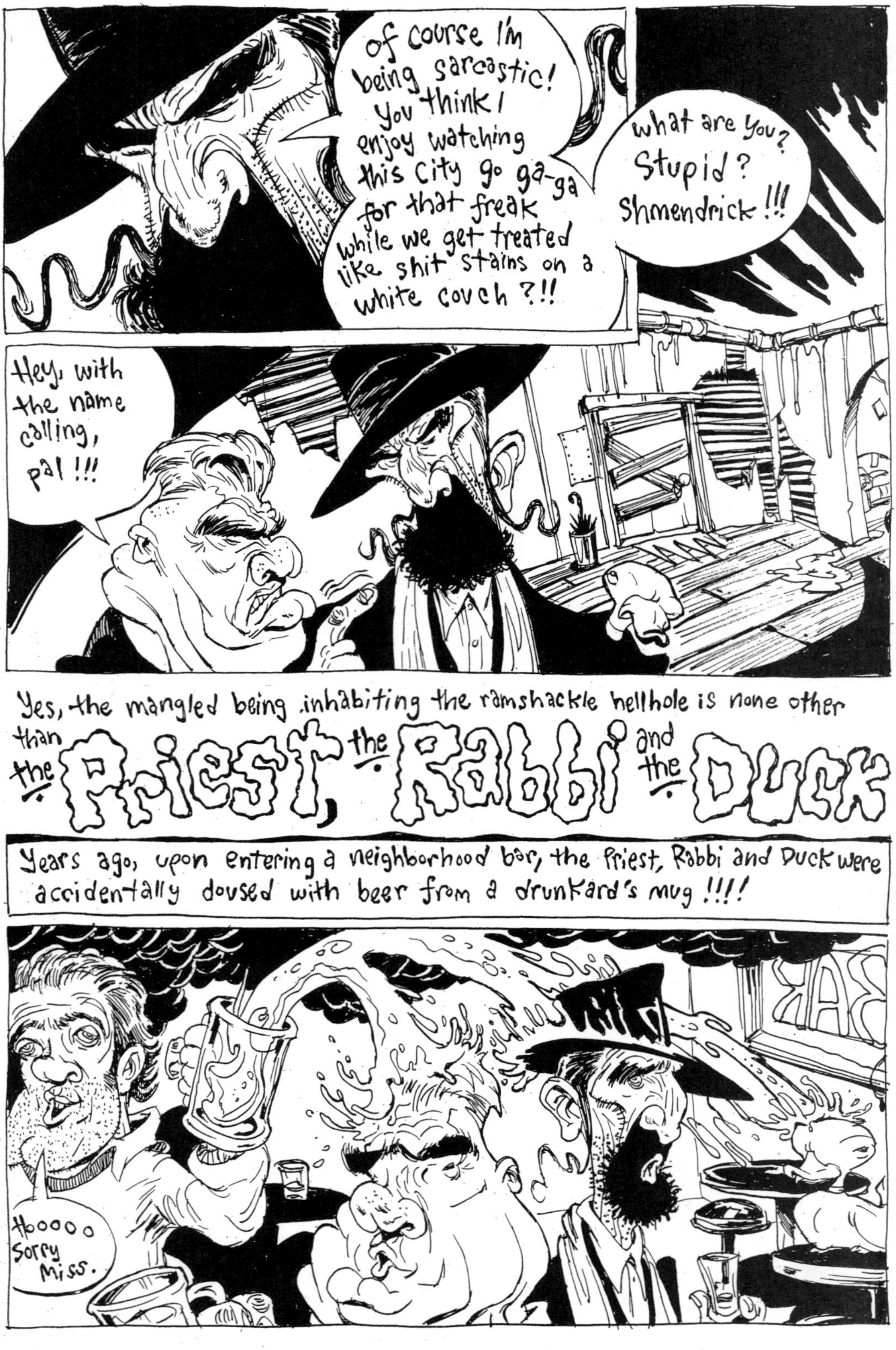
of course I'm being sarcastic! You think I enjoy watching this city go ga-ga for that freak while we get treated like shit stains on a white couch ?!!
what are you? Stupid? Shmendrick !!!
Hey, with the name calling, pal !!!
Yes, the mangled being inhabiting the ramshackle hellhole is none other than
the Priest, the Rabbi and the Duck
Years ago, upon entering a neighborhood bar, the Priest, Rabbi and Duck were accidentally doused with beer from a drunkard's mug !!!!
Hooooo Sorry Miss.

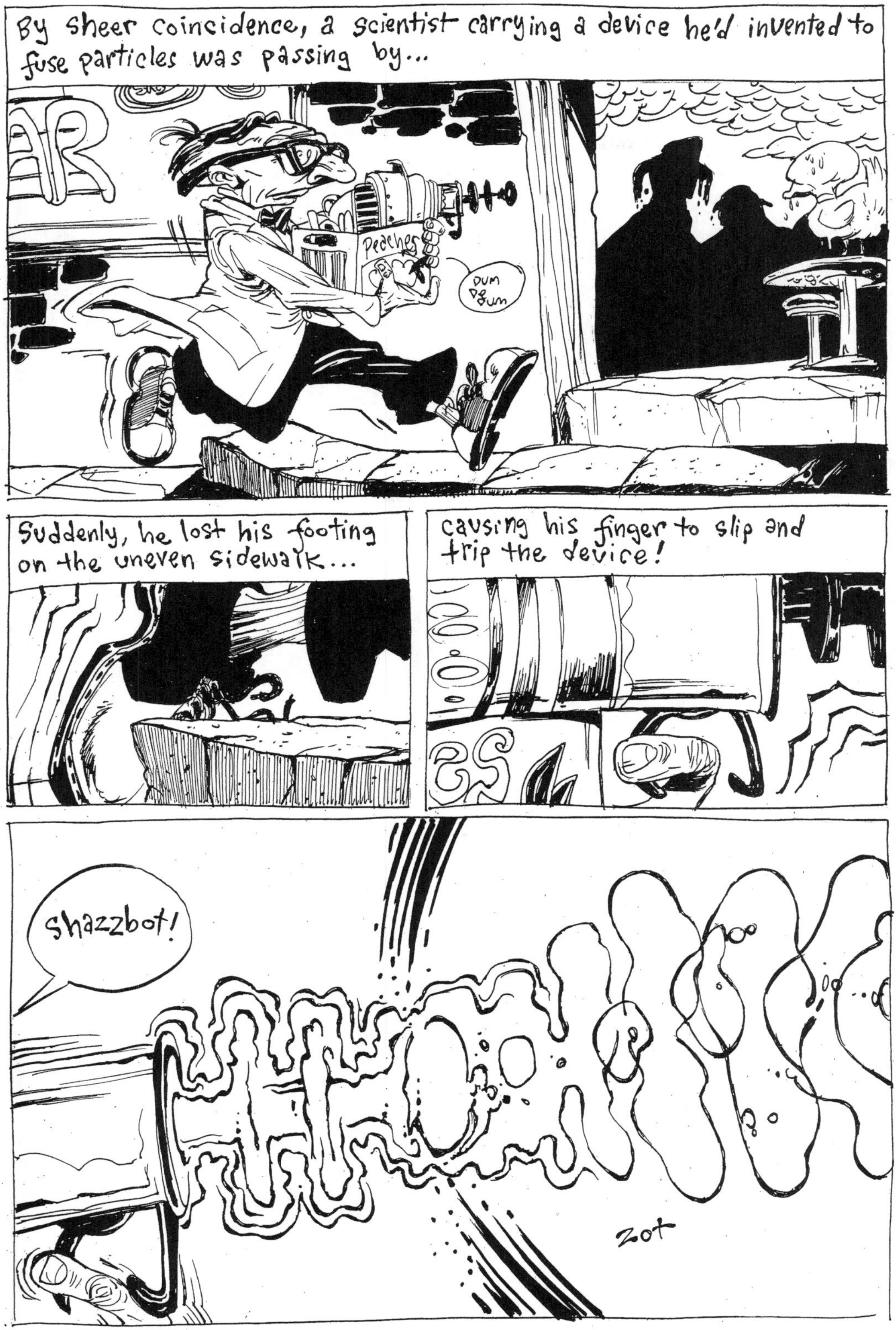
By sheer coincidence, a scientist carrying a device he'd invented to fuse particles was passing by...
Peaches
DUM DE DUM
Suddenly, he lost his footing on the uneven sidewalk...
causing his finger to slip and trip the device!
shazzbot!
zot

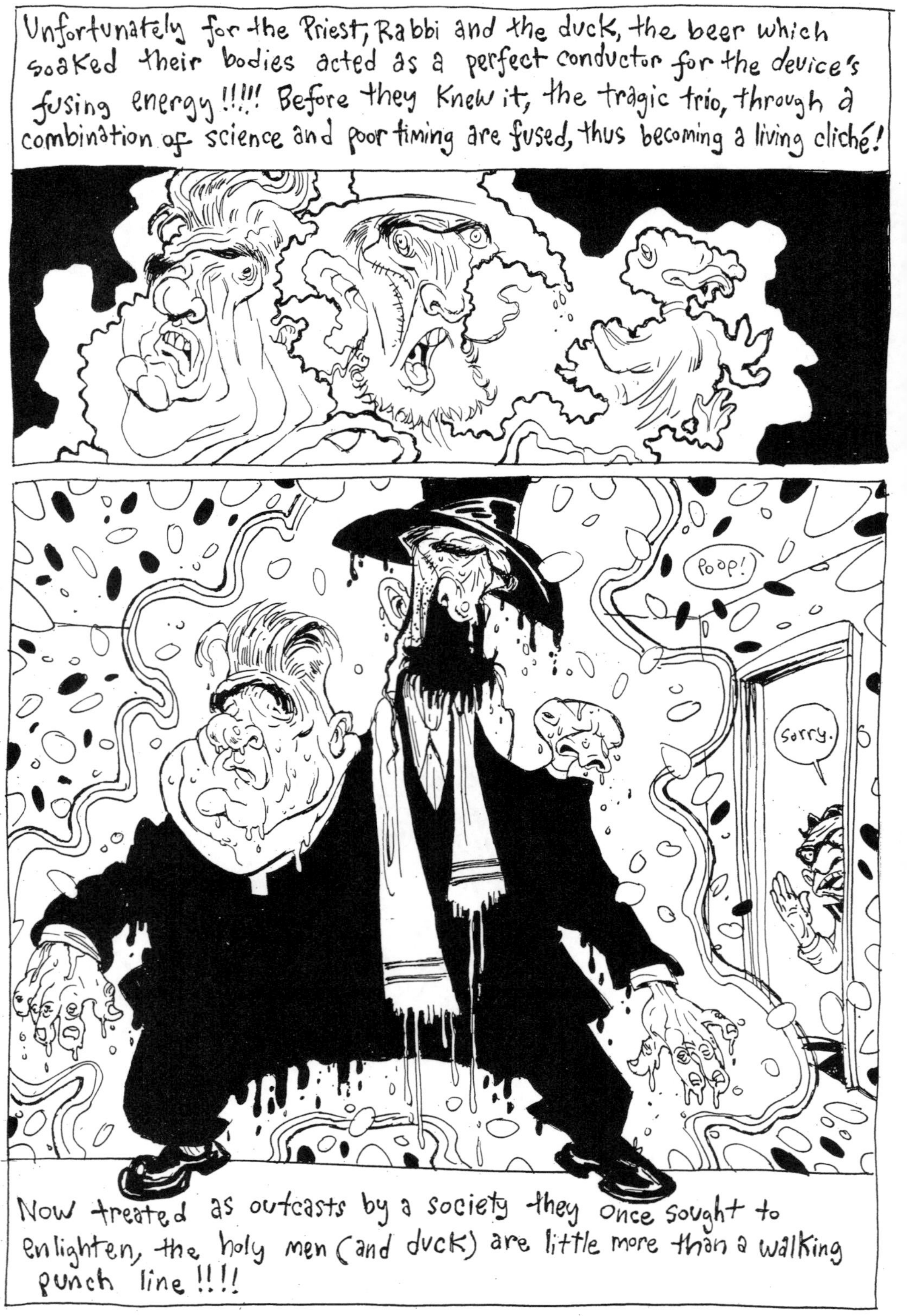
Unfortunately for the Priest, Rabbi and the duck, the beer which soaked their bodies acted as a perfect conductor for the device's fusing energy!!!!! Before they knew it, the tragic trio, through a combination of science and poor timing are fused, thus becoming a living cliché!
Poop!
Sorry.
Now treated as outcasts by a society they once sought to enlighten, the holy men (and duck) are little more than a walking punch line!!!!

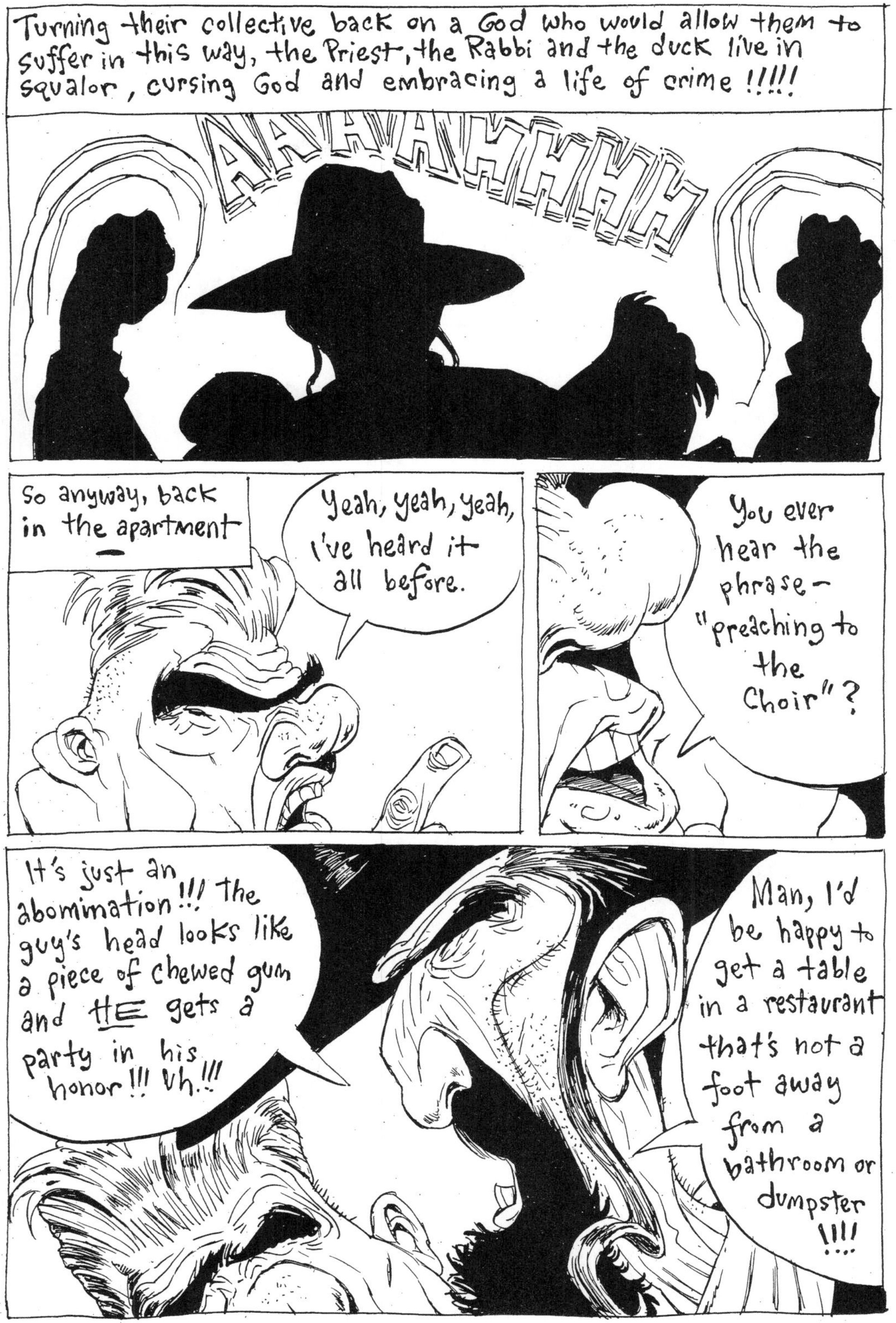
Turning their collective back on a God who would allow them to suffer in this way, the Priest, the Rabbi and the duck live in squalor, cursing God and embracing a life of crime !!!!!
AAAAHHHH
So anyway, back in the apartment —
Yeah, yeah, yeah, I've heard it all before.
You ever hear the phrase — "preaching to the Choir"?
It's just an abomination!!! the guy's head looks like a piece of chewed gum and HE gets a party in his honor!!! Uh!!!
Man, I'd be happy to get a table in a restaurant that's not a foot away from a bathroom or dumpster !!!!

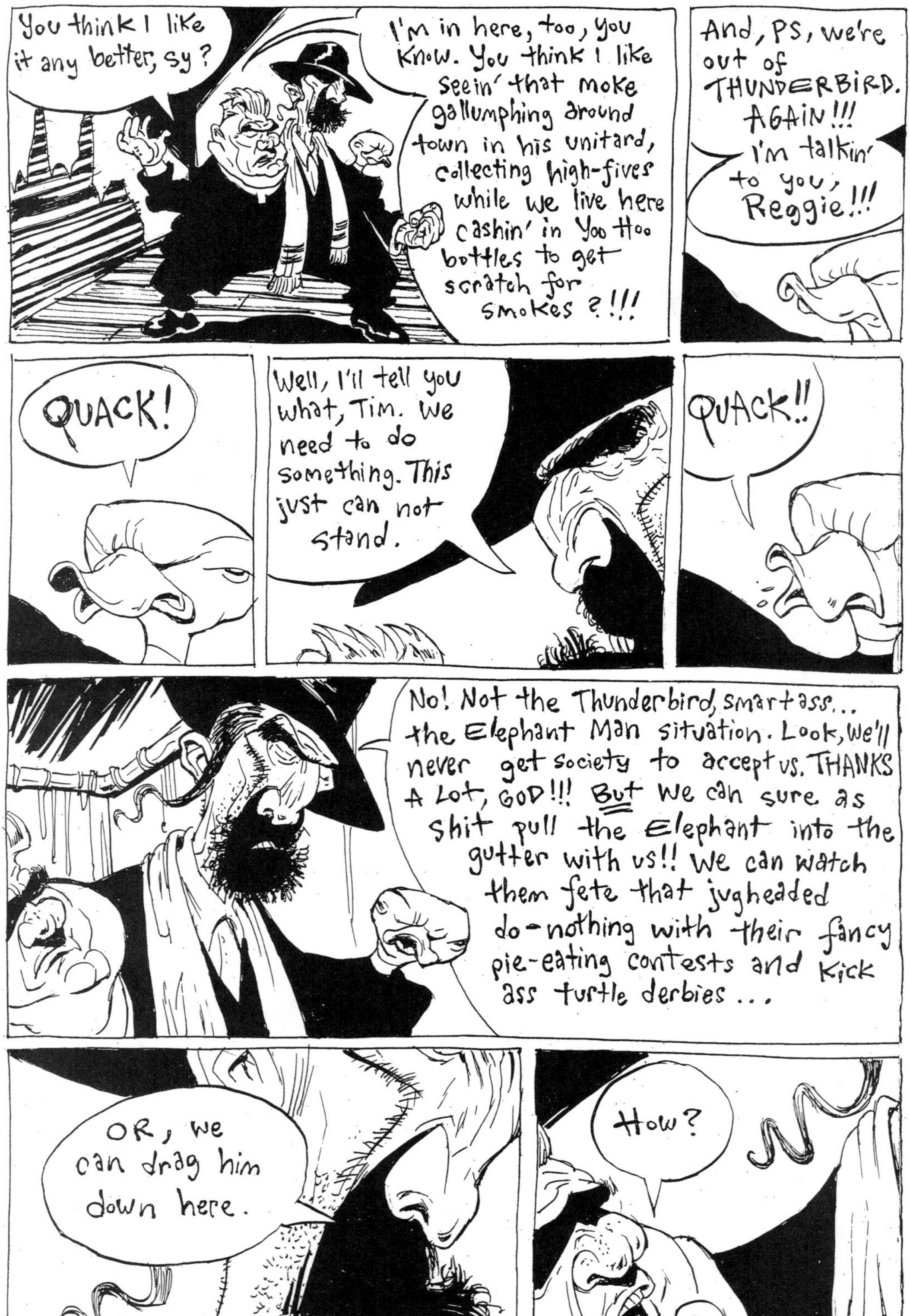
You think I like it any better, Sy?
I'm in here, too, you know. You think I like seein' that moke gallumphing around town in his unitard, collecting high-fives while we live here cashin' in Yoo Hoo bottles to get scratch for smokes?!!!
And, PS, we're out of THUNDERBIRD. AGAIN!!! I'm talkin' to you, Reggie!!!
QUACK!
Well, I'll tell you what, Tim. We need to do something. This just can not stand.
QUACK!!
No! Not the Thunderbird, smartass... the Elephant Man situation. Look, we'll never get society to accept us. THANKS A LOT, GOD!!! But we can sure as shit pull the Elephant into the gutter with us!! We can watch them fete that jugheaded do-nothing with their fancy pie-eating contests and kick ass turtle derbies...
OR, we can drag him down here.
How?

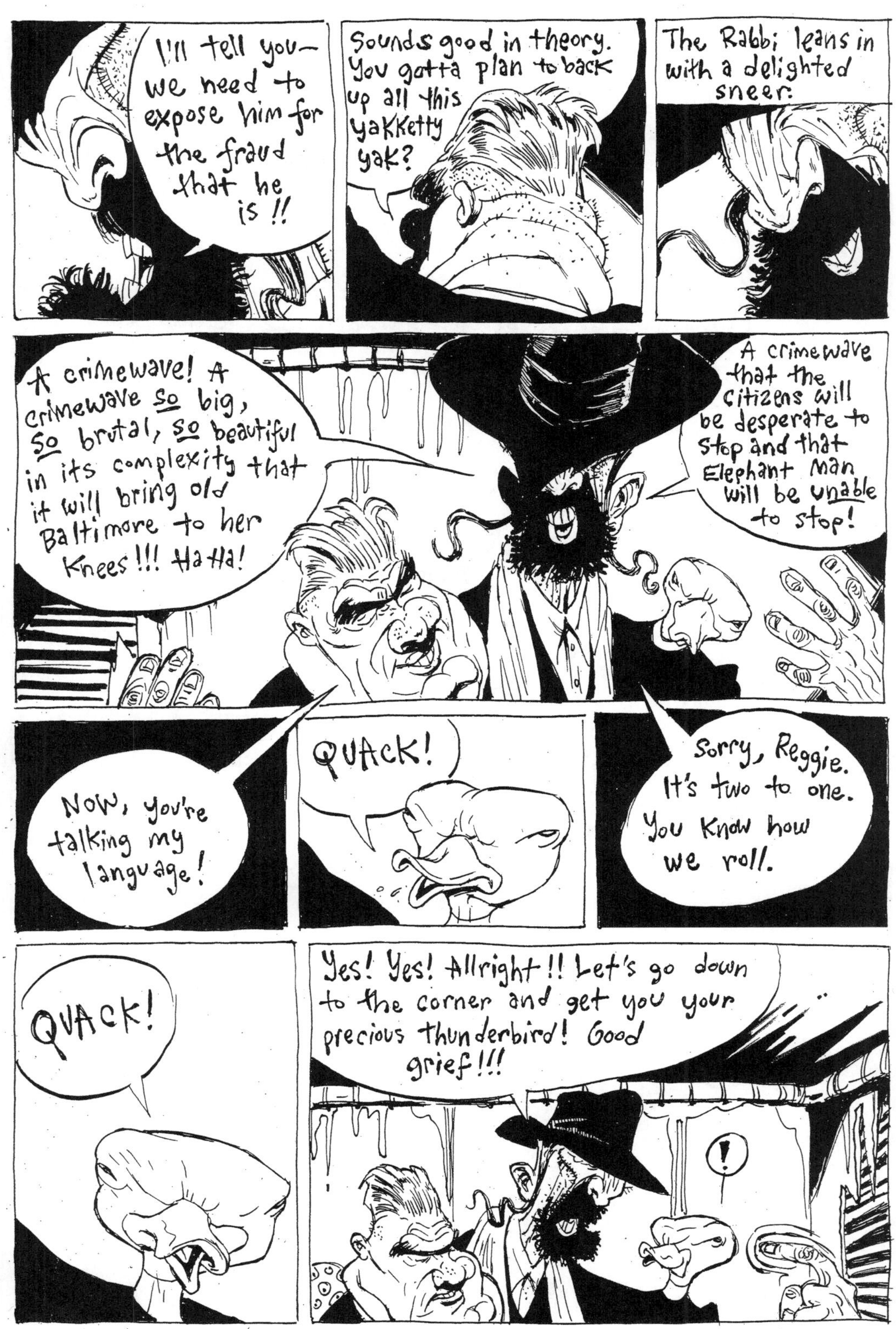

I'll tell you— we need to expose him for the fraud that he is !!
Sounds good in theory. You gotta plan to back up all this yakketty yak?
The Rabbi leans in with a delighted sneer.
A crimewave! A crimewave so big, so brutal, so beautiful in its complexity that it will bring old Baltimore to her Knees!!! HaHa!
A crimewave that the citizens will be desperate to stop and that Elephant Man will be unable to stop!
Now, you're talking my language!
QUACK!
Sorry, Reggie. It's two to one. You know how we roll.
QUACK!
Yes! Yes! Allright!! Let's go down to the corner and get you your precious thunderbird! Good grief!!!
!

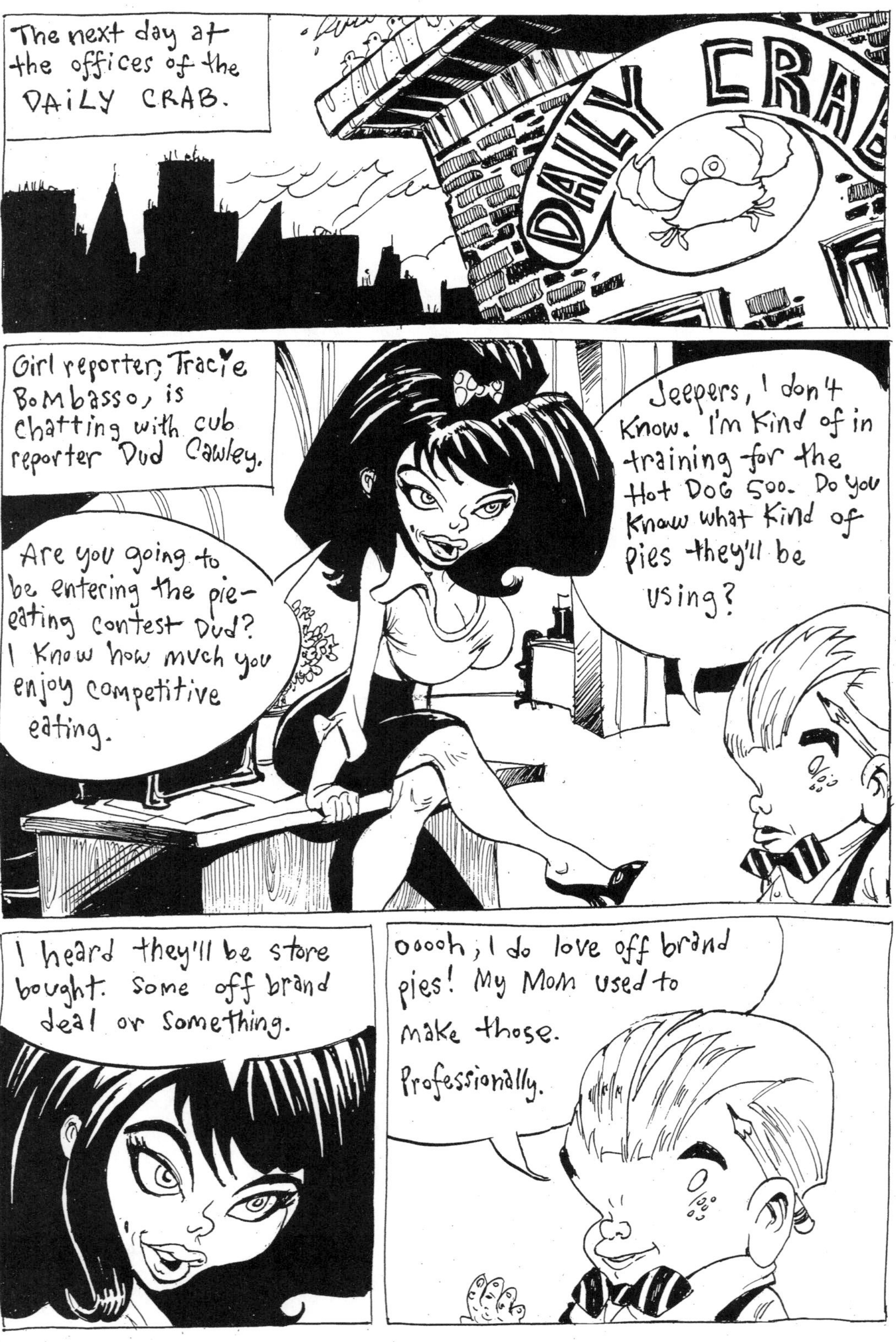
The next day at the offices of the DAILY CRAB.
DAILY CRAB
Girl reporter, Tracie Bombasso, is chatting with cub reporter Dud Cawley.
Are you going to be entering the pie-eating contest Dud? I know how much you enjoy competitive eating.
Jeepers, I don't know. I'm kind of in training for the Hot Dog 500. Do you know what kind of pies they'll be using?
I heard they'll be store bought. Some off brand deal or something.
Ooooh, I do love off brand pies! My Mom used to make those. Professionally.

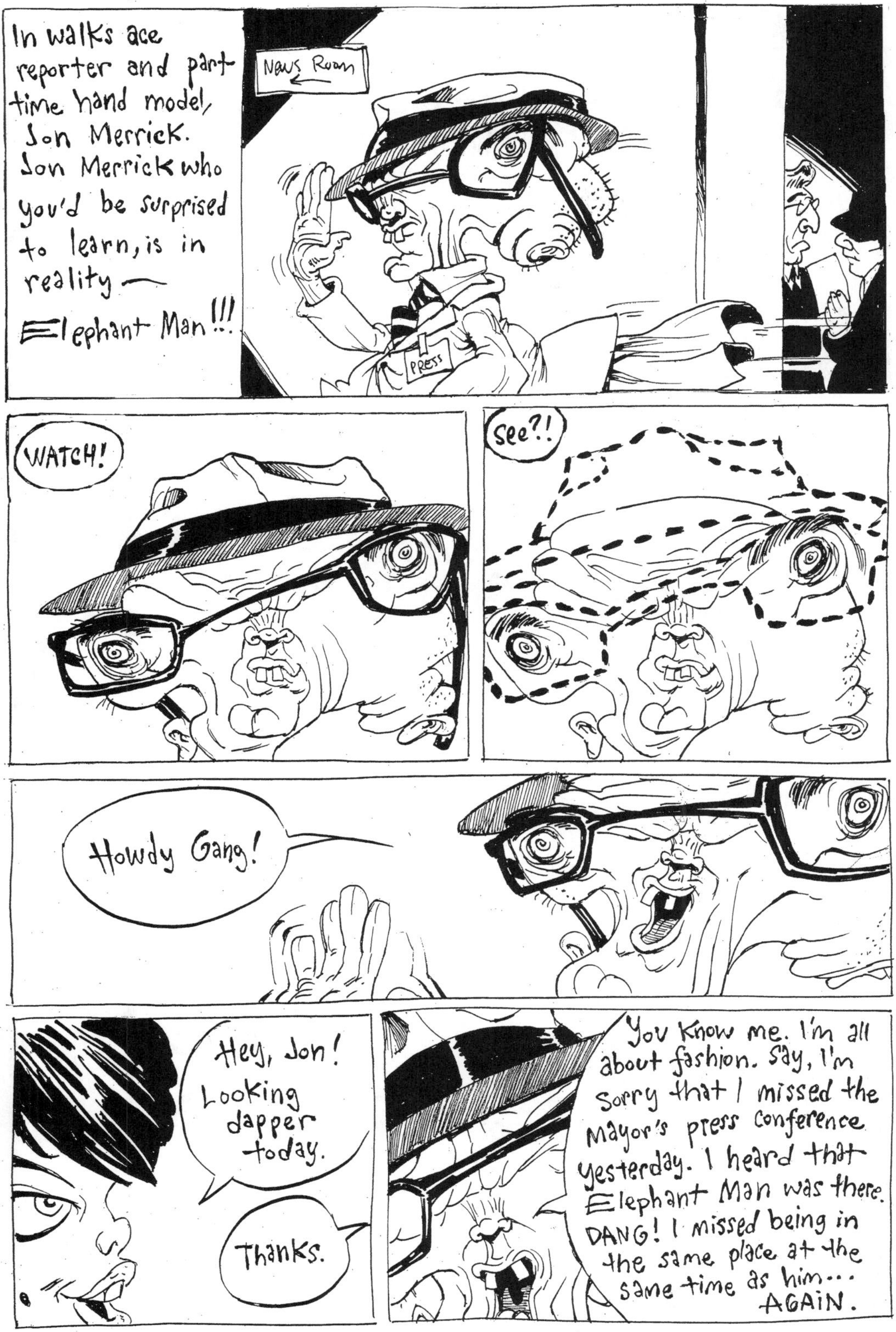
In walks ace reporter and part time hand model, Jon Merrick. Jon Merrick who you'd be surprised to learn, is in reality — Elephant Man!!!
News Room
PRESS
WATCH!
See?!
Howdy Gang!
Hey, Jon! Looking dapper today.
Thanks.
You know me. I'm all about fashion. Say, I'm sorry that I missed the mayor's press conference yesterday. I heard that Elephant Man was there. DANG! I missed being in the same place at the same time as him... AGAIN.

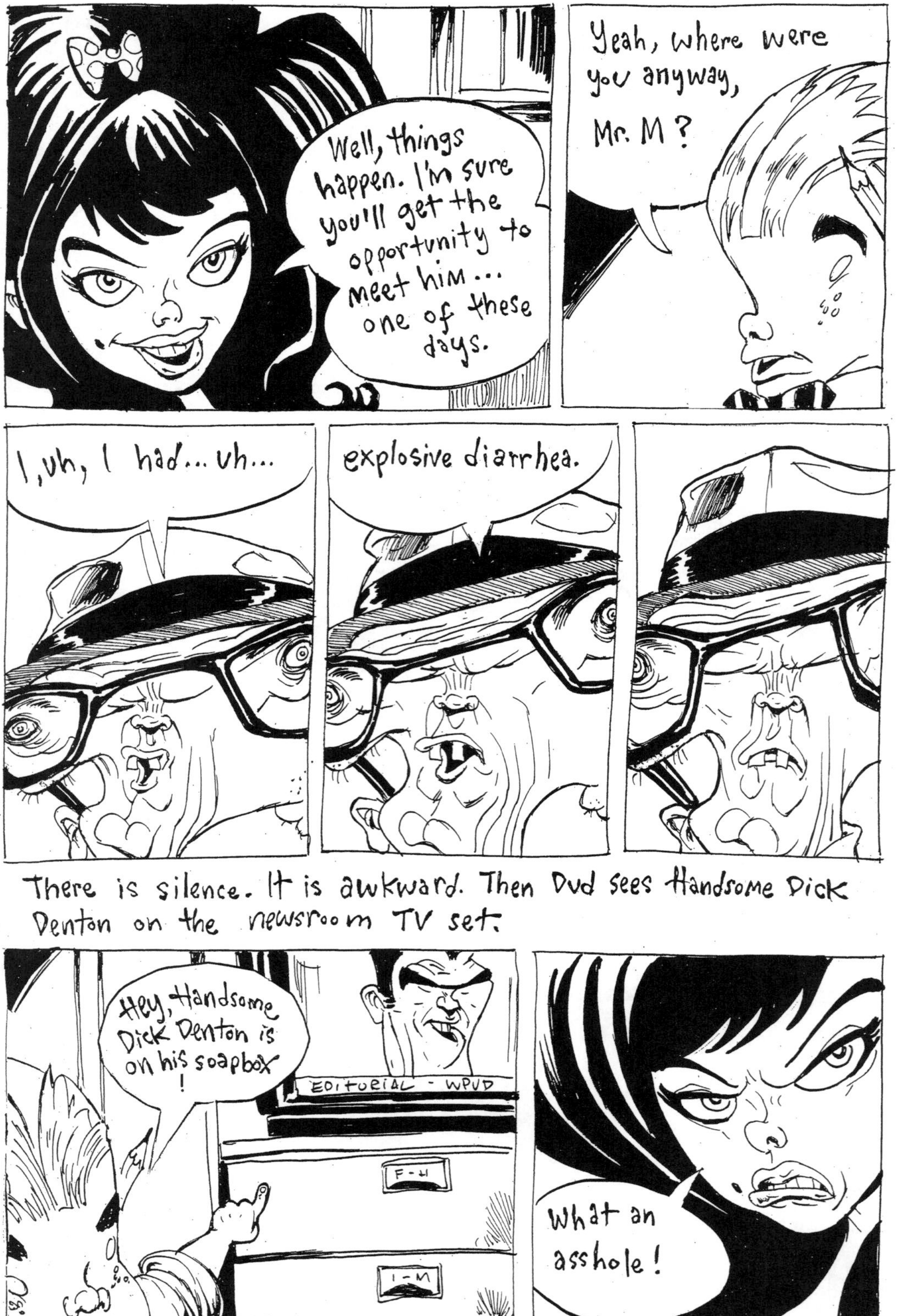
Well, things happen. I'm sure you'll get the opportunity to meet him... one of these days.
Yeah, where were you anyway, Mr. M?
I, uh, I had... uh...
explosive diarrhea.
There is silence. It is awkward. Then Dud sees Handsome Dick Denton on the newsroom TV set.
Hey, Handsome Dick Denton is on his soapbox!
EDITORIAL - WPUD
F-H
I-M
What an asshole!

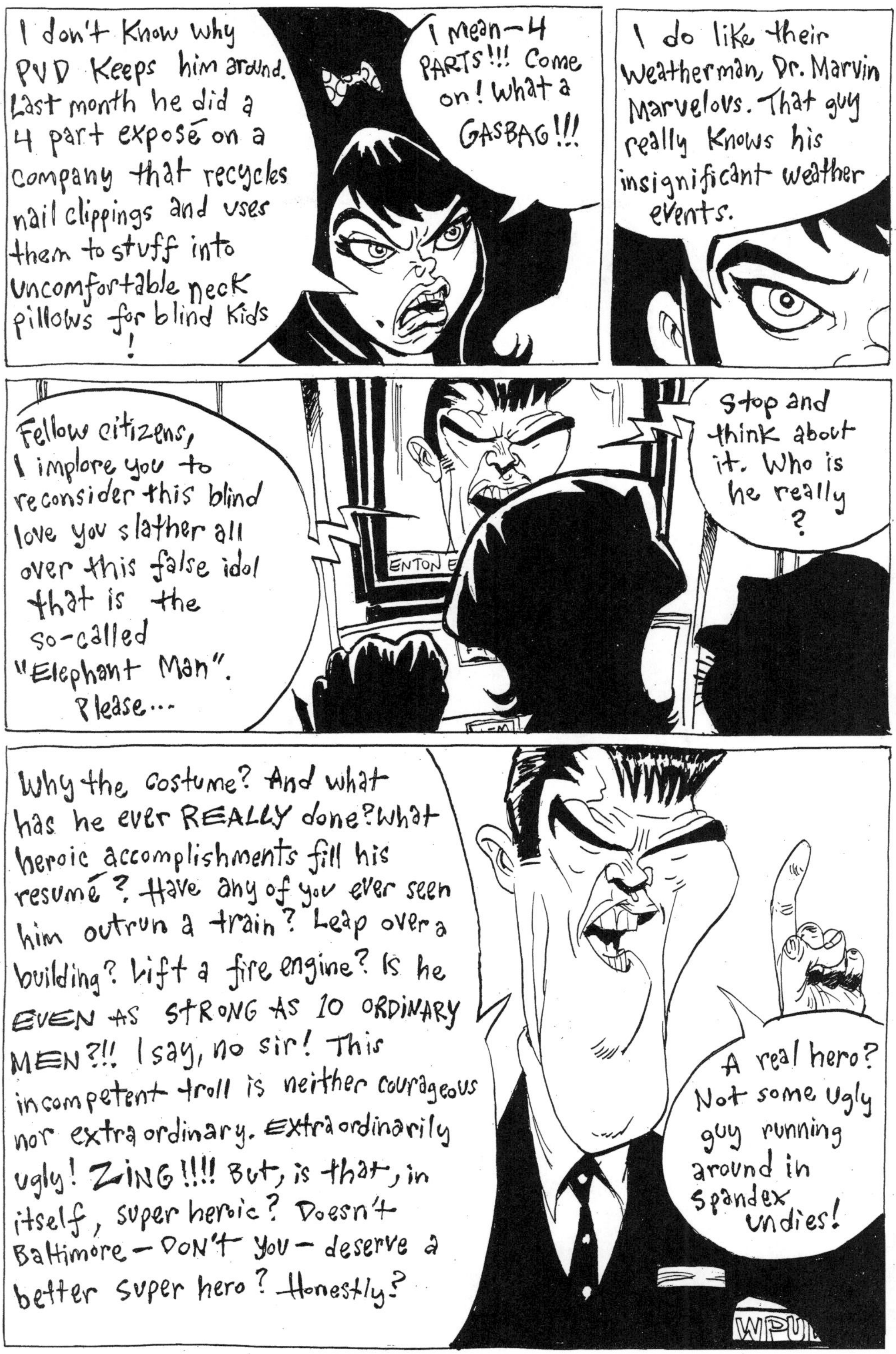
I don't Know why PVD Keeps him around. Last month he did a 4 part exposé on a company that recycles nail clippings and uses them to stuff into uncomfortable neck pillows for blind kids!
I mean—4 PARTS!!! Come on! What a GASBAG!!!
I do like their weatherman, Dr. Marvin Marvelous. That guy really Knows his insignificant weather events.
Fellow citizens, I implore you to reconsider this blind love you slather all over this false idol that is the so-called "Elephant Man". Please...
Stop and think about it. Who is he really?
Why the costume? And what has he ever REALLY done? What heroic accomplishments fill his resumé? Have any of you ever seen him outrun a train? Leap over a building? Lift a fire engine? Is he EVEN AS STRONG AS 10 ORDINARY MEN?!! I say, no sir! This incompetent troll is neither courageous nor extraordinary. Extraordinarily ugly! ZING!!!! But, is that, in itself, super heroic? Doesn't Baltimore—DON'T YOU—deserve a better super hero? Honestly?
A real hero? Not some ugly guy running around in spandex undies!

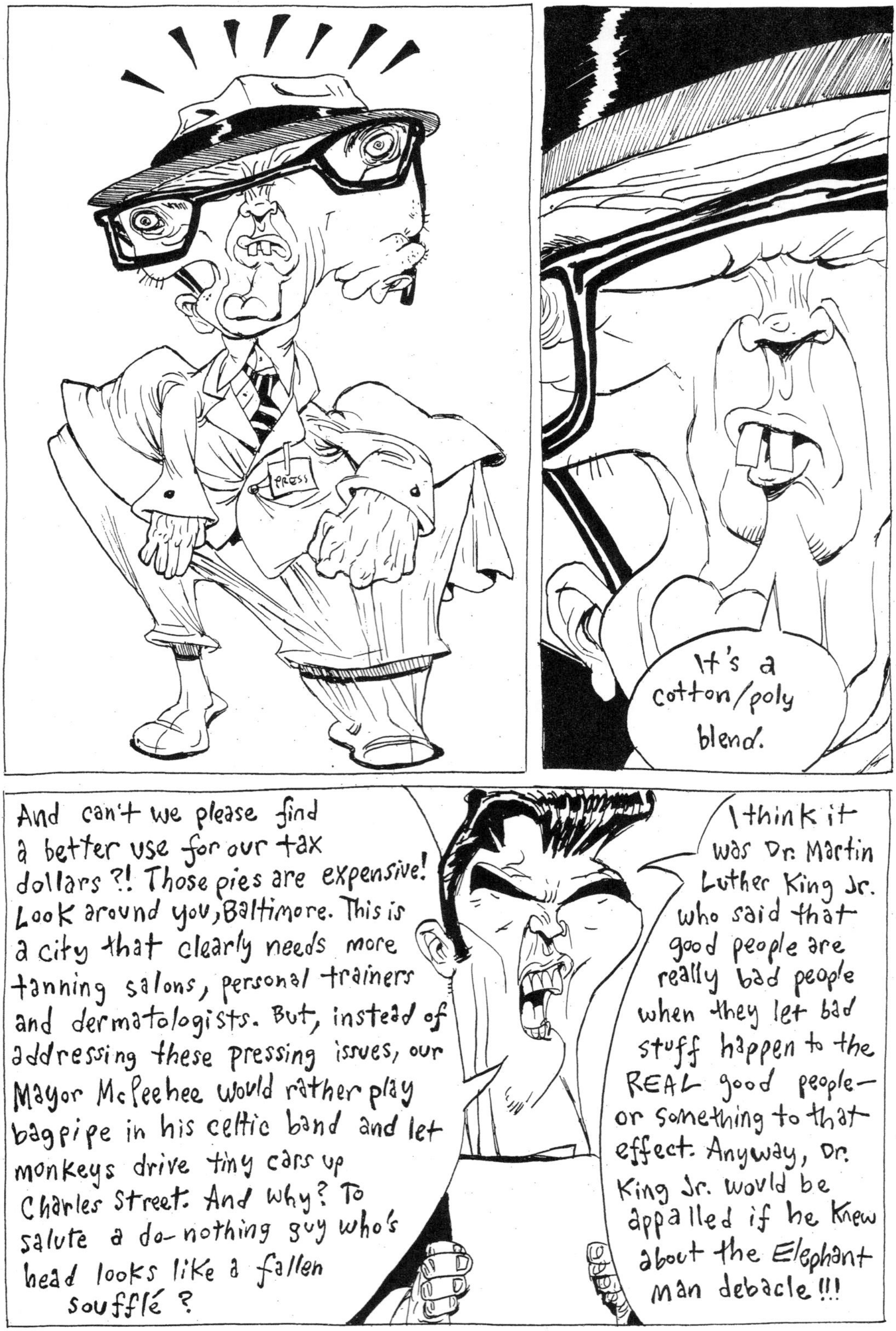
PRESS
It's a cotton/poly blend.
And can't we please find a better use for our tax dollars?! Those pies are expensive! Look around you, Baltimore. This is a city that clearly needs more tanning salons, personal trainers and dermatologists. But, instead of addressing these pressing issues, our Mayor McPeehee would rather play bagpipe in his celtic band and let monkeys drive tiny cars up Charles Street. And why? To salute a do-nothing guy who's head looks like a fallen soufflé?
I think it was Dr. Martin Luther King Jr. who said that good people are really bad people when they let bad stuff happen to the REAL good people—or something to that effect. Anyway, Dr. King Jr. would be appalled if he knew about the Elephant Man debacle!!!

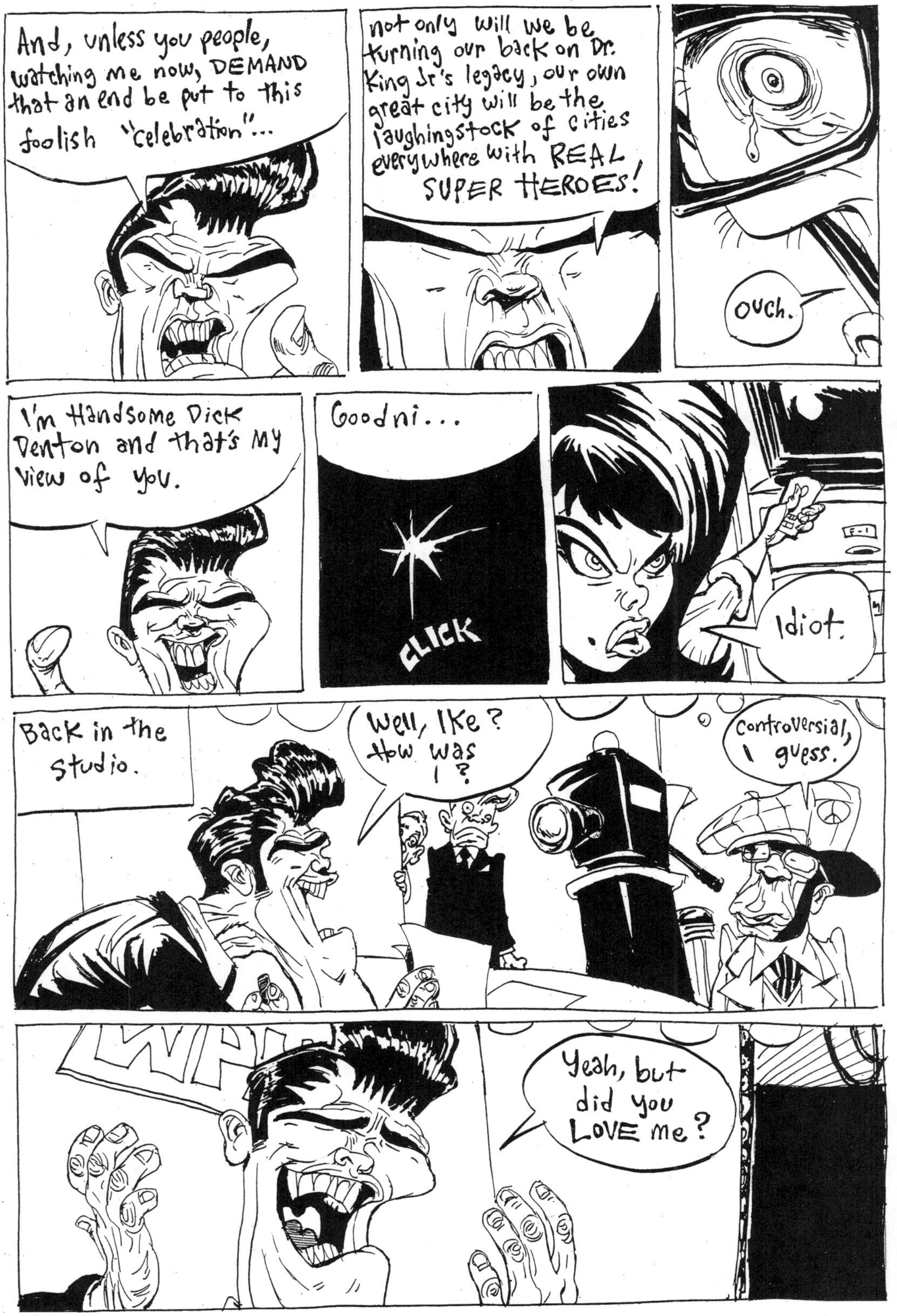
And, unless you people, watching me now, DEMAND that an end be put to this foolish "celebration"...
not only will we be turning our back on Dr. King Jr's legacy, our own great city will be the laughingstock of cities everywhere with REAL SUPER HEROES!
Ouch.
I'm Handsome Dick Denton and that's my view of you.
Goodni...
CLICK
Idiot.
Back in the studio.
Well, Ike? How was I?
Controversial, I guess.
Yeah, but did you LOVE me?

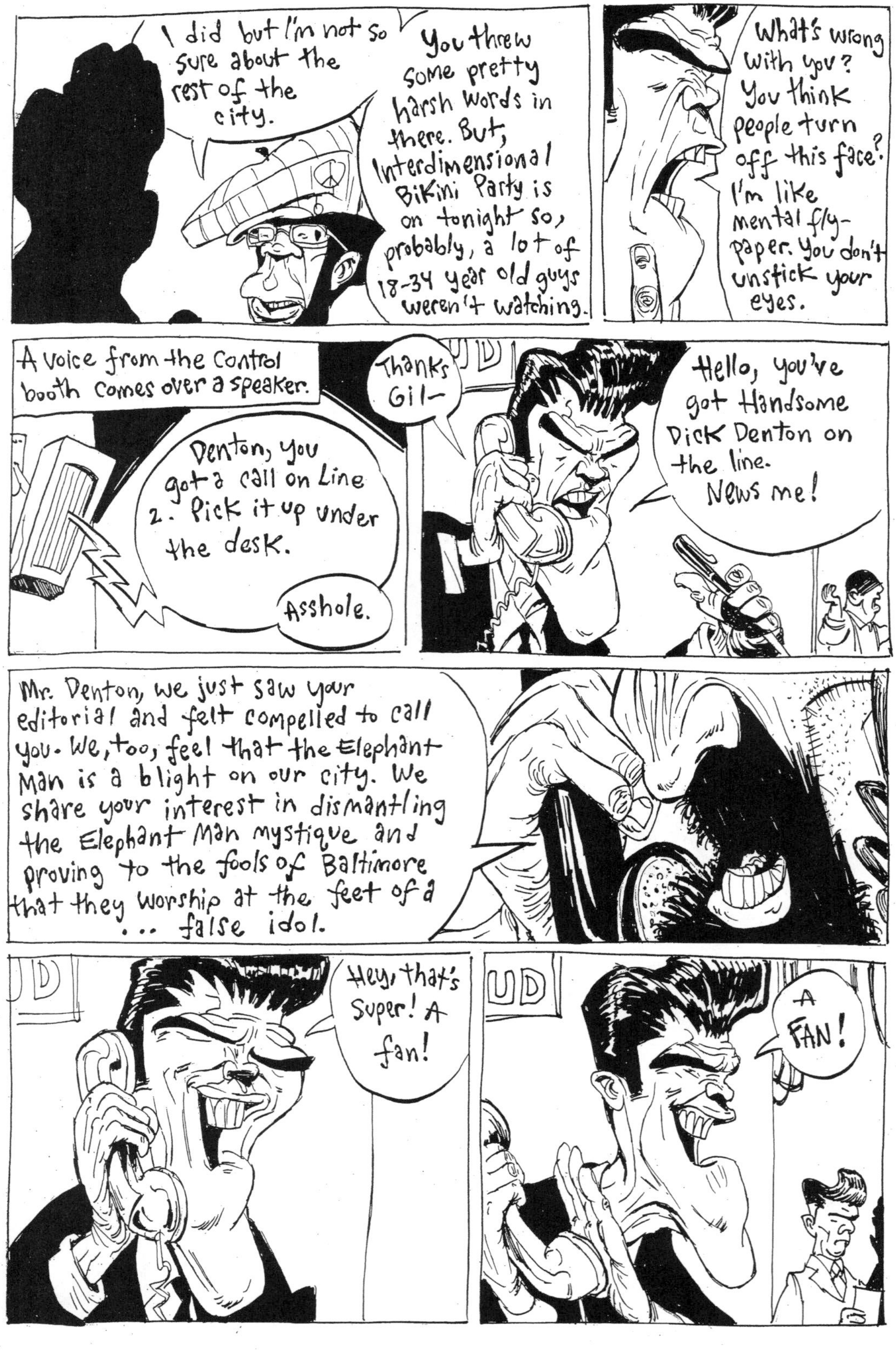
I did but I'm not so sure about the rest of the city.
You threw some pretty harsh words in there. But, Interdimensional Bikini Party is on tonight so, probably, a lot of 18-34 year old guys weren't watching.
What's wrong with you? You think people turn off this face? I'm like mental fly-paper. You don't unstick your eyes.
A voice from the control booth comes over a speaker.
Denton, you got a call on Line 2. Pick it up under the desk.
Asshole.
Thanks Gil—
UD
Hello, you've got Handsome Dick Denton on the line. News me!
Mr. Denton, we just saw your editorial and felt compelled to call you. We, too, feel that the Elephant Man is a blight on our city. We share your interest in dismantling the Elephant Man mystique and proving to the fools of Baltimore that they worship at the feet of a ... false idol.
UD
Hey, that's super! A fan!
UD
A FAN!

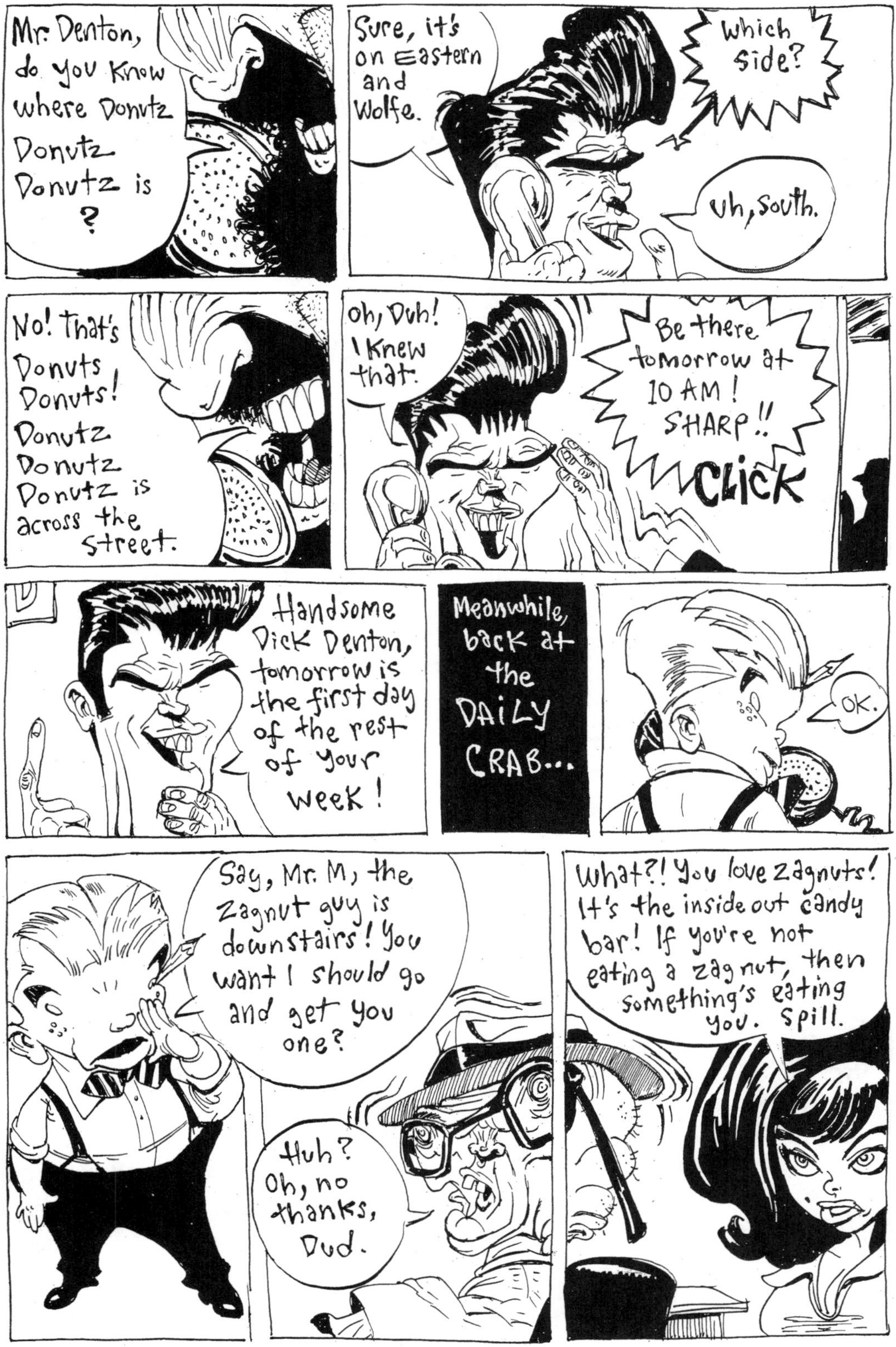
Mr. Denton, do you know where Donutz Donutz Donutz is ?
Sure, it's on Eastern and Wolfe.
Which side?
Uh, south.
No! That's Donuts Donuts! Donutz Donutz Donutz is across the street.
Oh, Duh! I knew that.
Be there tomorrow at 10 AM! SHARP!!
CLICK
Handsome Dick Denton, tomorrow is the first day of the rest of your week!
Meanwhile, back at the DAILY CRAB...
OK.
Say, Mr. M, the Zagnut guy is downstairs! You want I should go and get you one?
Huh? Oh, no thanks, Dud.
What?! You love Zagnuts! It's the inside out candy bar! If you're not eating a Zagnut, then something's eating you. Spill.

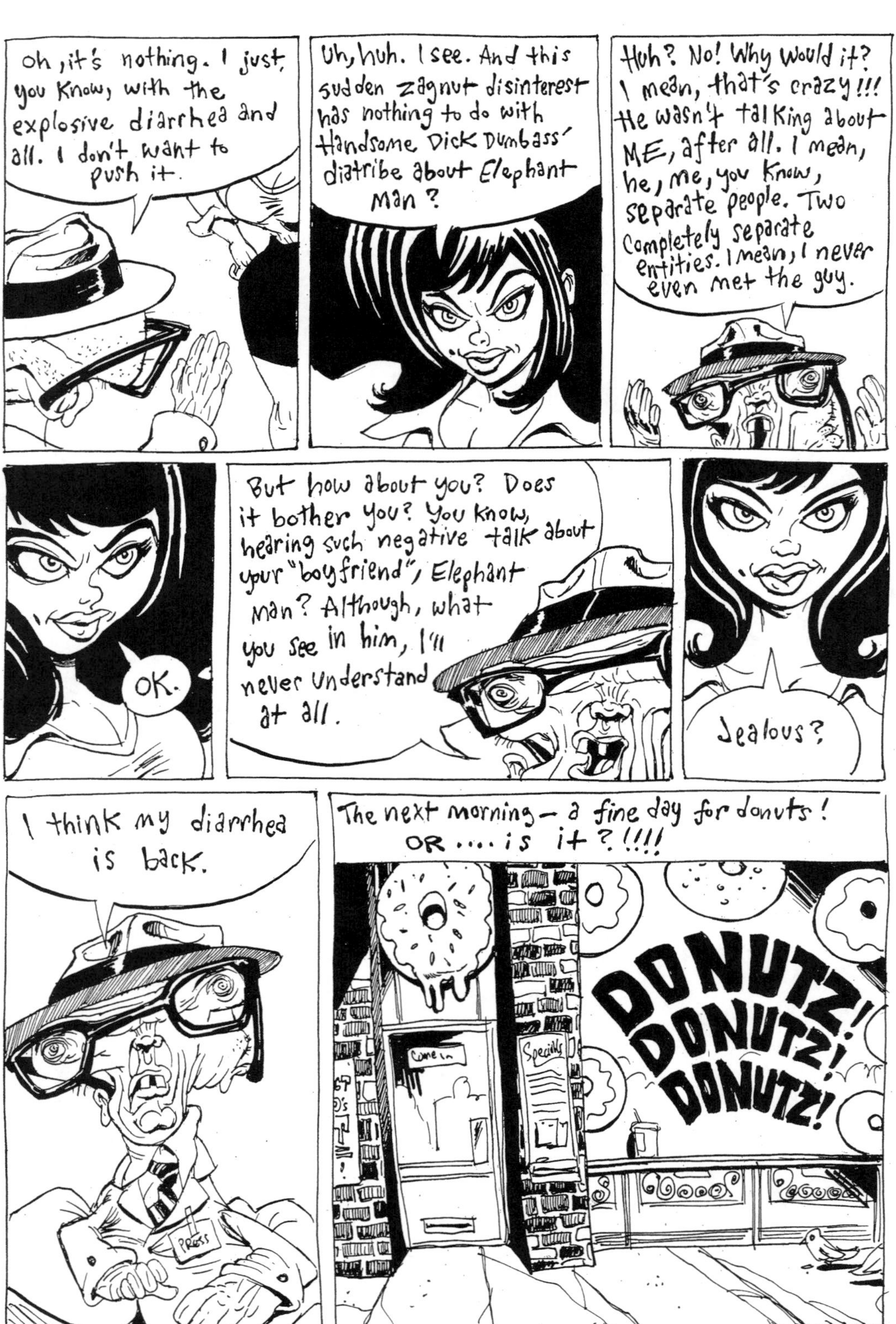
Oh, it's nothing. I just, you know, with the explosive diarrhea and all. I don't want to push it.
Uh, huh. I see. And this sudden Zagnut disinterest has nothing to do with Handsome Dick Dumbass' diatribe about Elephant Man?
Huh? No! Why would it? I mean, that's crazy!!! He wasn't talking about ME, after all. I mean, he, me, you know, separate people. Two completely separate entities. I mean, I never even met the guy.
OK.
But how about you? Does it bother you? You know, hearing such negative talk about your "boyfriend", Elephant Man? Although, what you see in him, I'll never understand at all.
Jealous?
I think my diarrhea is back.
The next morning — a fine day for donuts! OR.... is it?!!!!
Come in
Specials
PRESS
DONUTZ! DONUTZ! DONUTZ!

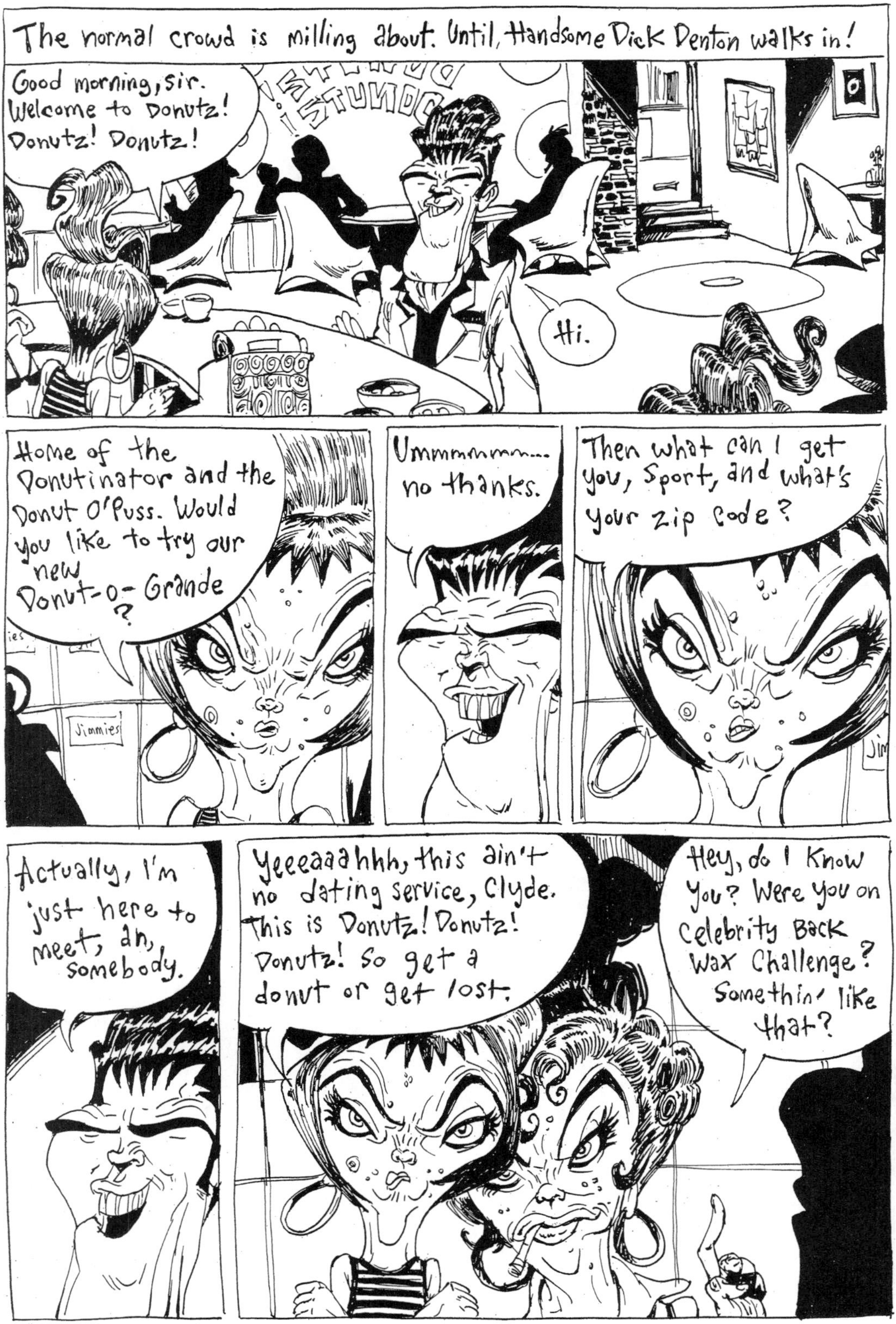
The normal crowd is milling about. Until, Handsome Dick Denton walks in!
Good morning, sir. Welcome to Donutz! Donutz! Donutz!
Hi.
Home of the Donutinator and the Donut O'Puss. Would you like to try our new Donut-o-Grande?
Jimmies
Ummmmmm... no thanks.
Then what can I get you, Sport, and what's your zip code?
Actually, I'm just here to meet, ah, somebody.
Yeeeaaahhh, this ain't no dating service, Clyde. This is Donutz! Donutz! Donutz! So get a donut or get lost.
Hey, do I know you? Were you on Celebrity Back Wax Challenge? Somethin' like that?

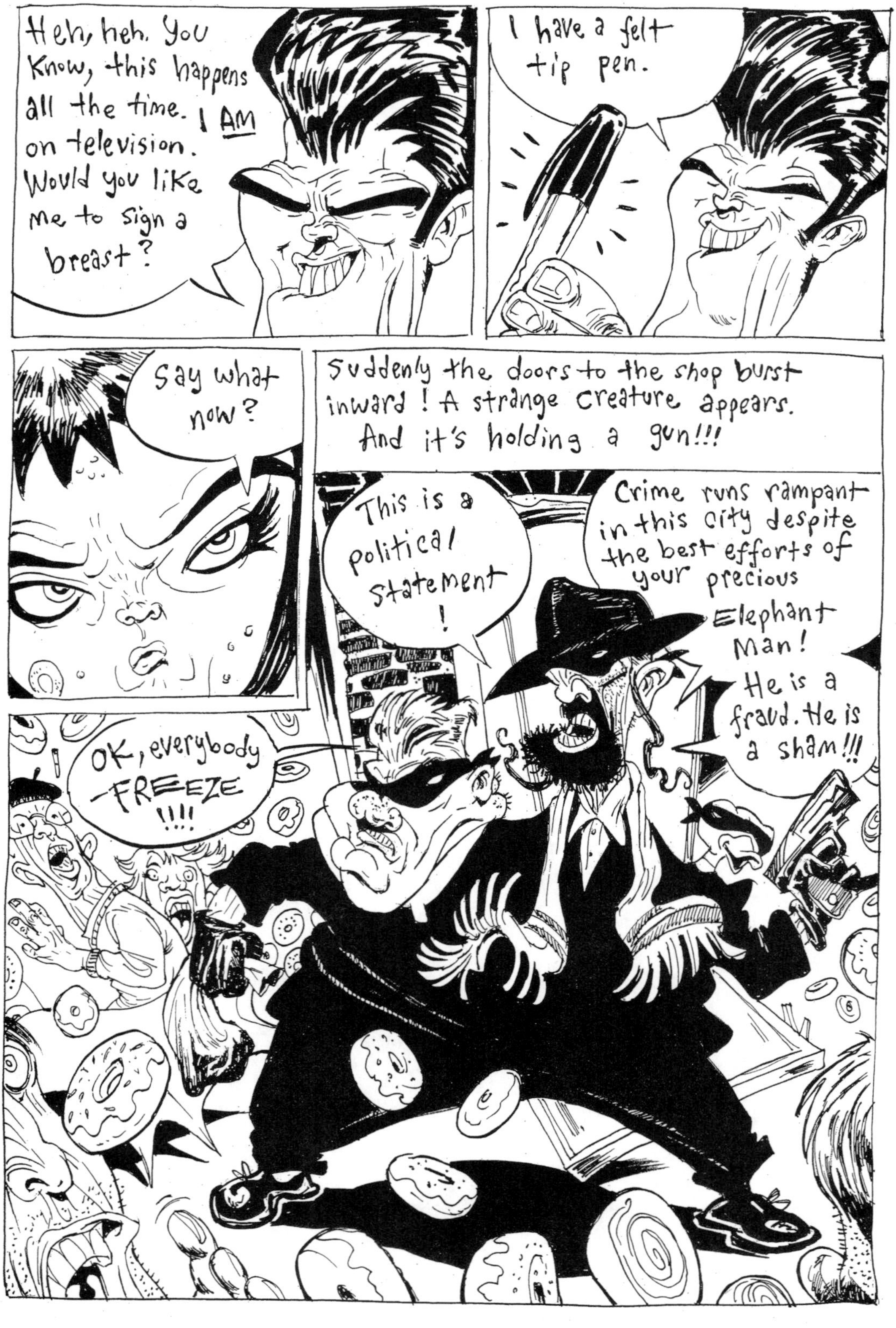
Heh, heh. You Know, this happens all the time. I AM on television. Would you like me to sign a breast?
I have a felt tip pen.
Say what now?
Suddenly the doors to the shop burst inward! A strange creature appears. And it's holding a gun!!!
This is a political statement!
Crime runs rampant in this city despite the best efforts of your precious Elephant Man!
He is a fraud. He is a sham!!!
OK, everybody FREEZE!!!!

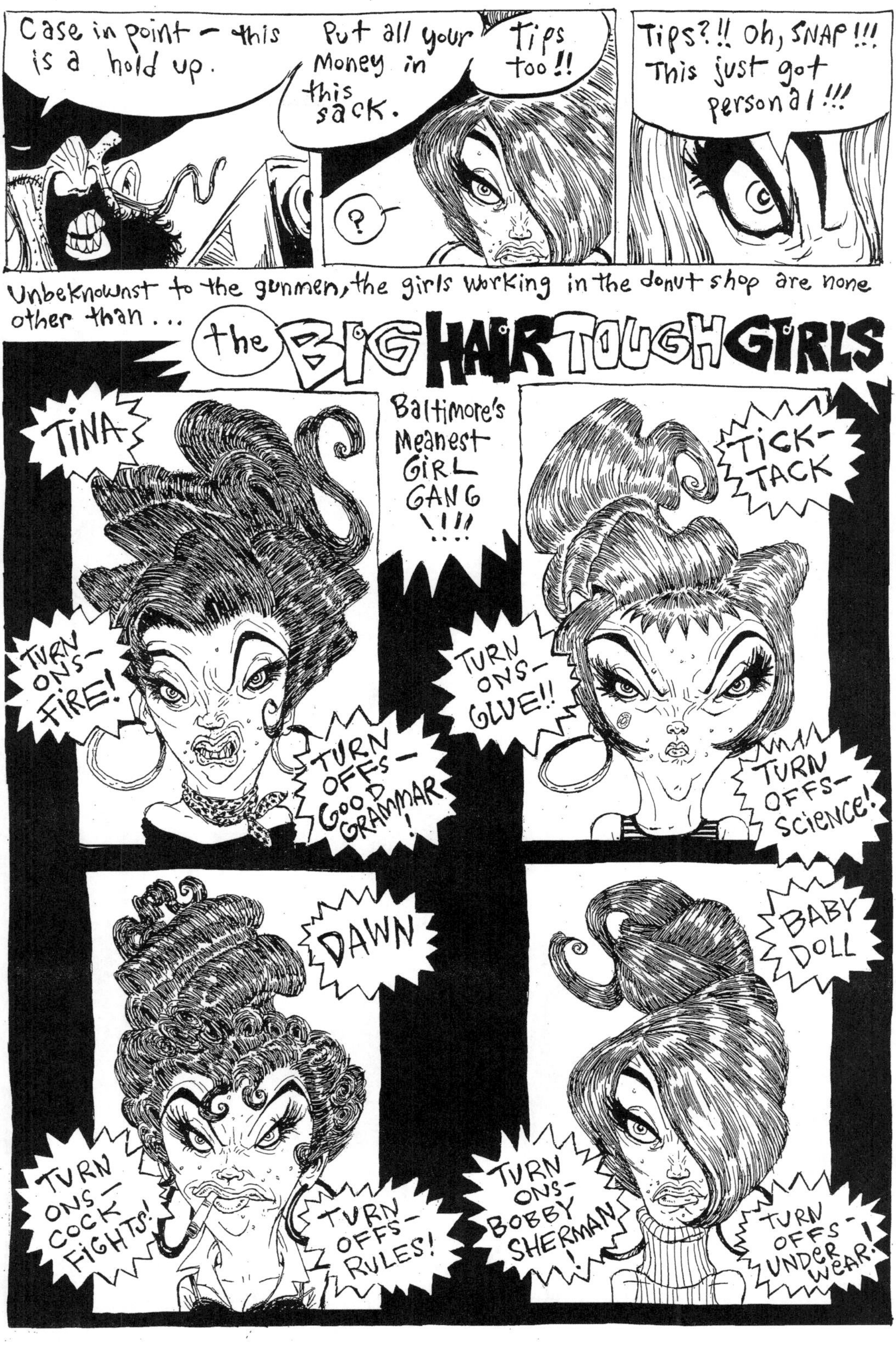
Case in point — this is a hold up.
Put all your Money in this sack.
?
Tips too!!
Tips?!! Oh, SNAP!!! This just got personal!!!
Unbeknownst to the gunmen, the girls working in the donut shop are none other than...
the BIG HAIR TOUGH GIRLS
Baltimore's Meanest GIRL GANG !!!!
TINA
TURN ONS- FIRE!
TURN OFFS- GOOD GRAMMAR!
TICK-TACK
TURN ONS- GLUE!!
TURN OFFS- SCIENCE!
DAWN
TURN ONS- COCK FIGHTS!
TURN OFFS- RULES!
BABY DOLL
TURN ONS- BOBBY SHERMAN!
TURN OFFS- UNDER WEAR!

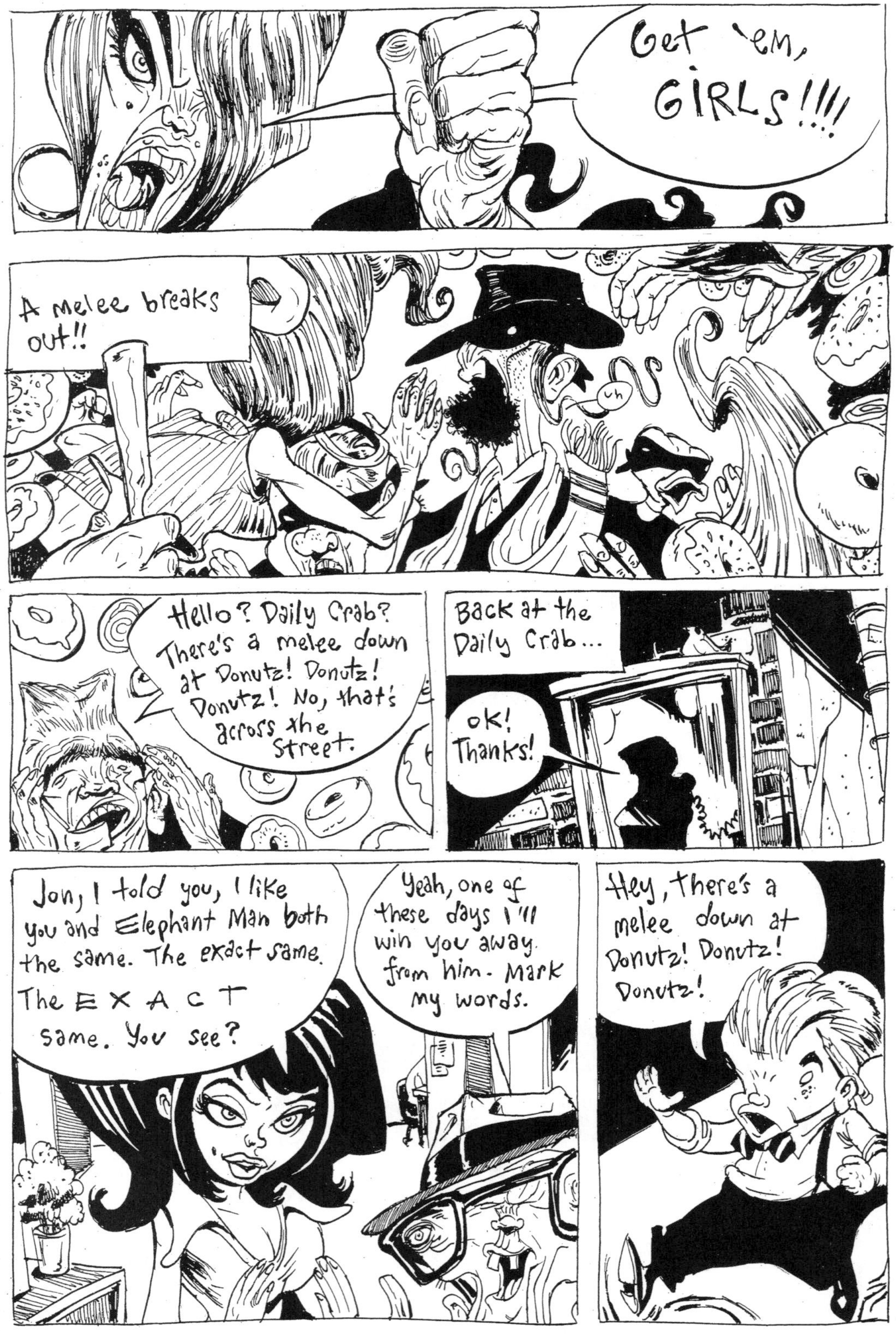
Get 'em, GIRLS!!!!
A melee breaks out!!
uh
Hello? Daily Crab? There's a melee down at Donutz! Donutz! Donutz! No, that's across the street.
Back at the Daily Crab...
ok! Thanks!
Jon, I told you, I like you and Elephant Man both the same. The exact same. The E X A C T same. You see?
Yeah, one of these days I'll win you away from him. Mark my words.
Hey, there's a melee down at Donutz! Donutz! Donutz!

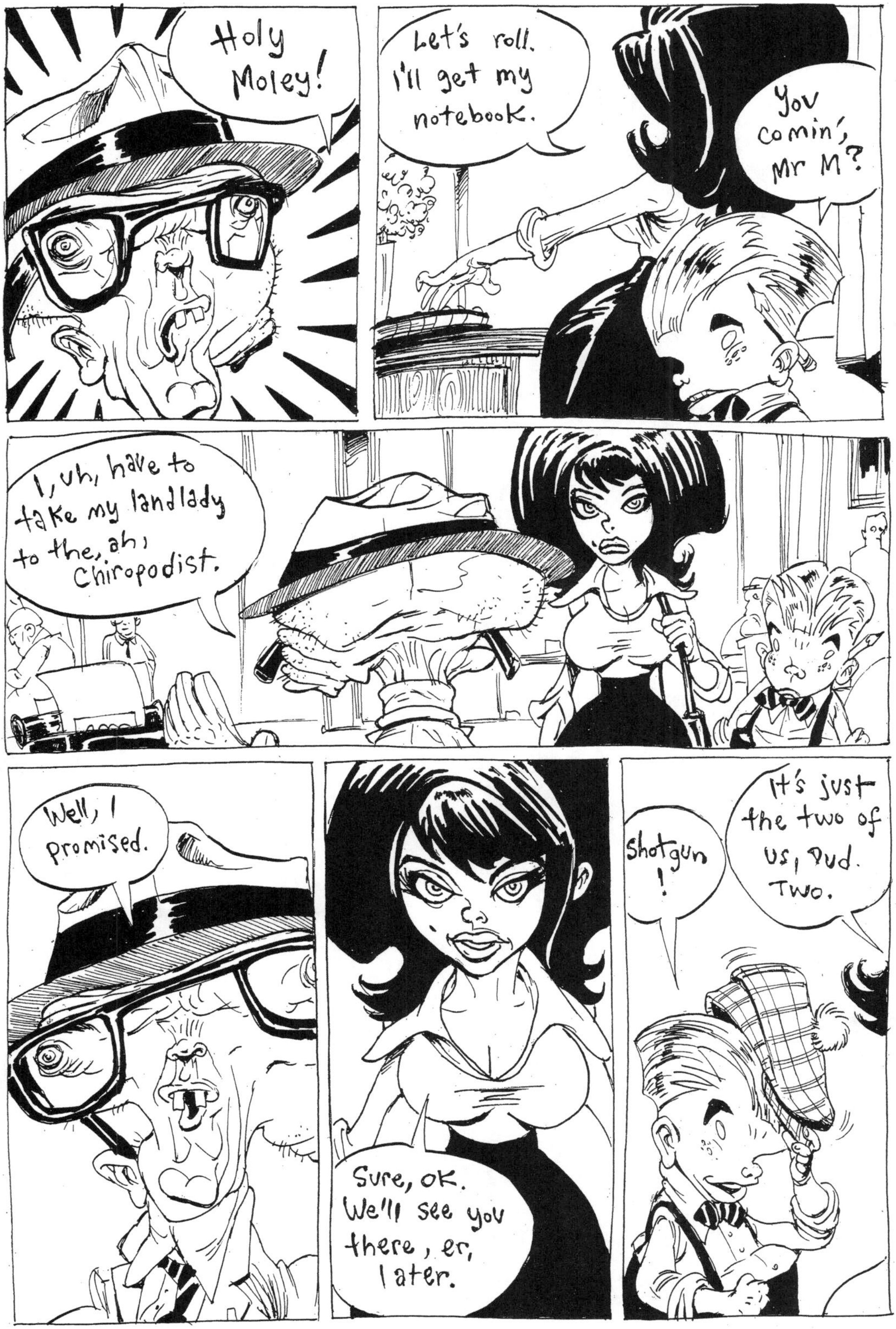
Holy Moley!
Let's roll. I'll get my notebook.
You comin', Mr M?
I, uh, have to take my landlady to the, ah, Chiropodist.
Well, I promised.
Sure, OK. We'll see you there, er, later.
Shotgun!
It's just the two of us, Dud. Two.

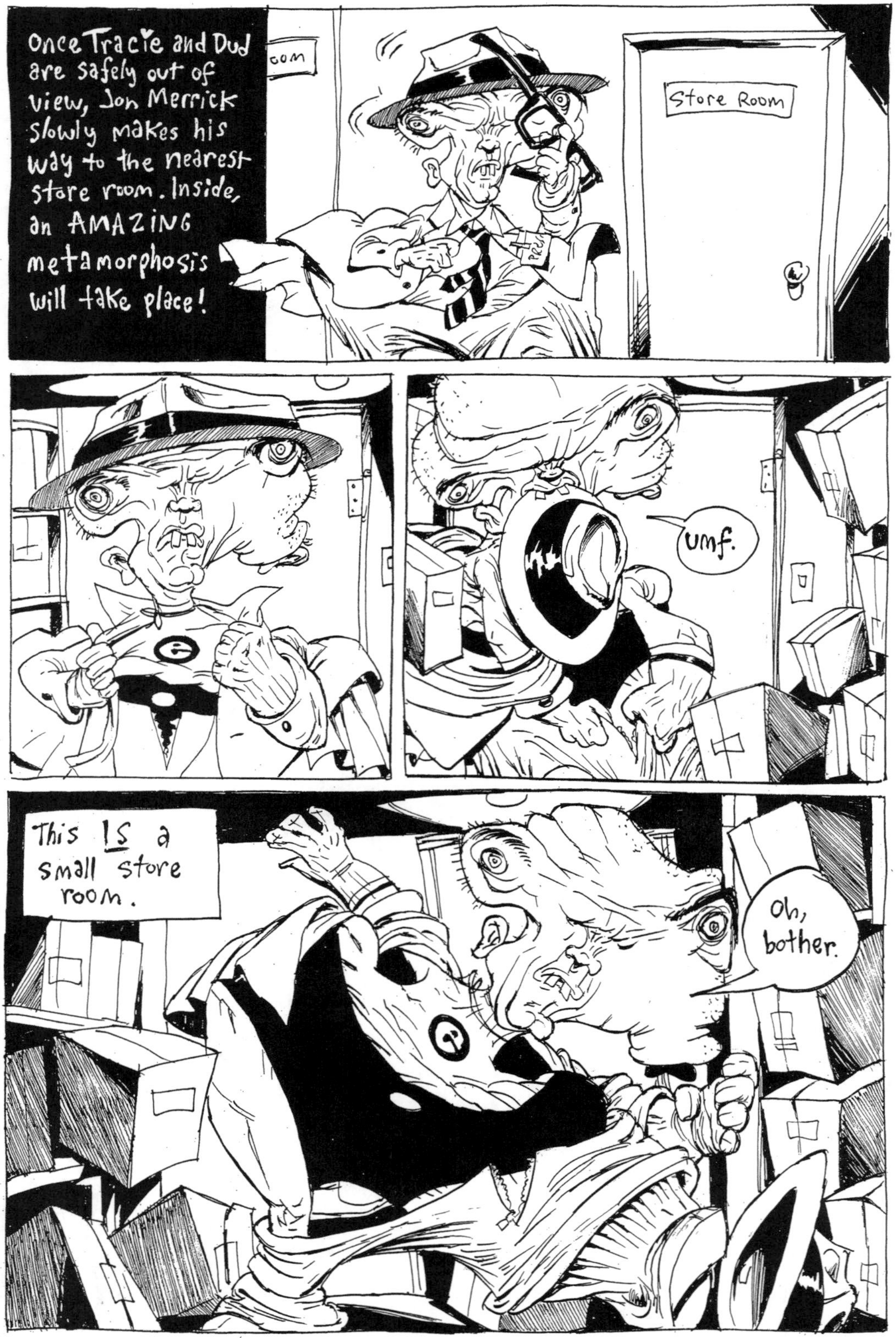
Once Tracie and Dud are safely out of view, Jon Merrick slowly makes his way to the nearest store room. Inside, an AMAZING metamorphosis will take place!
Store Room
umf.
This IS a small store room.
Oh, bother.

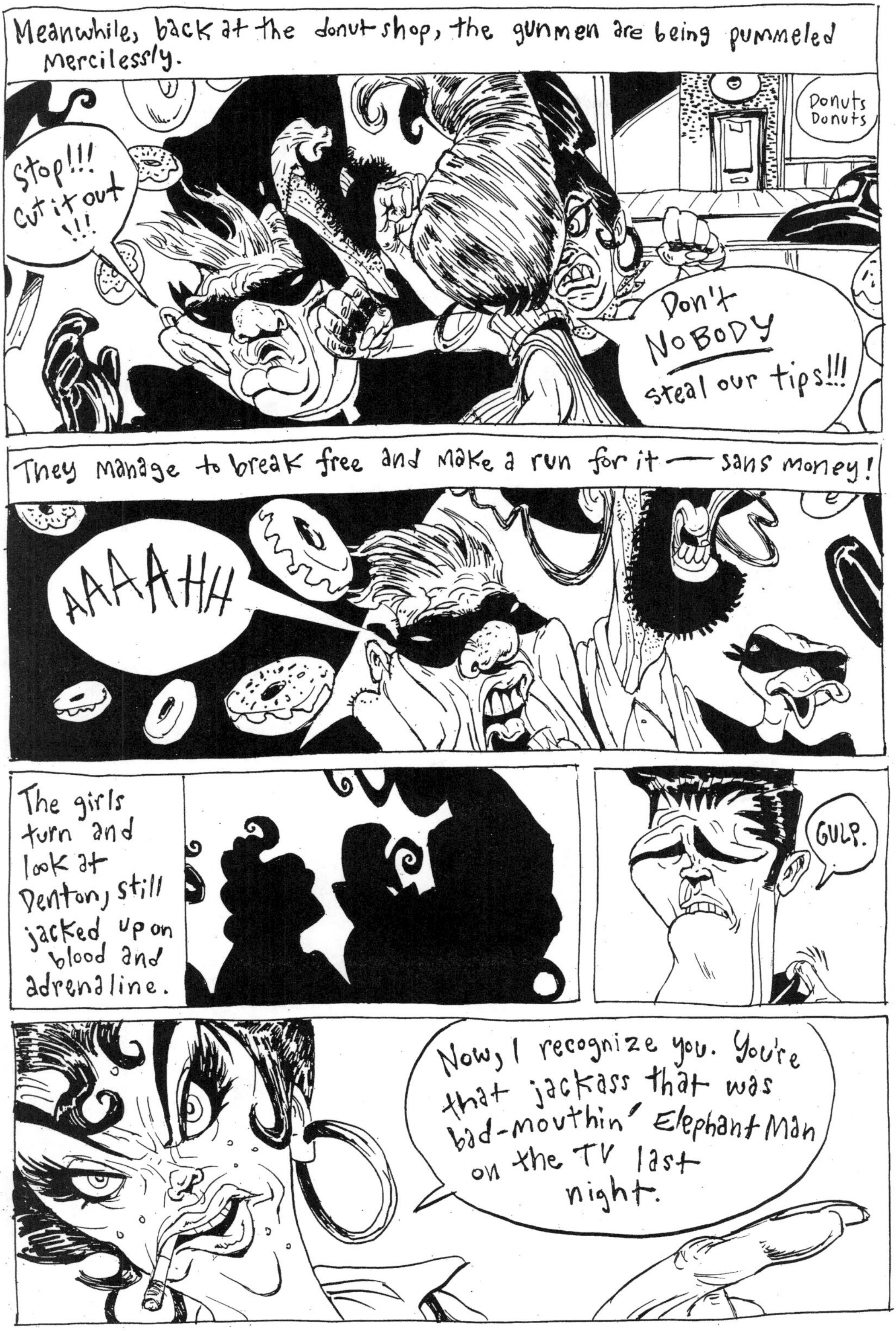
Meanwhile, back at the donut shop, the gunmen are being pummeled mercilessly.
Donuts Donuts
Stop!!! Cut it out !!!
Don't NOBODY steal our tips!!!
They manage to break free and make a run for it — sans money!
AAAAHH
The girls turn and look at Denton, still jacked up on blood and adrenaline.
GULP.
Now, I recognize you. You're that jackass that was bad-mouthin' Elephant Man on the TV last night.

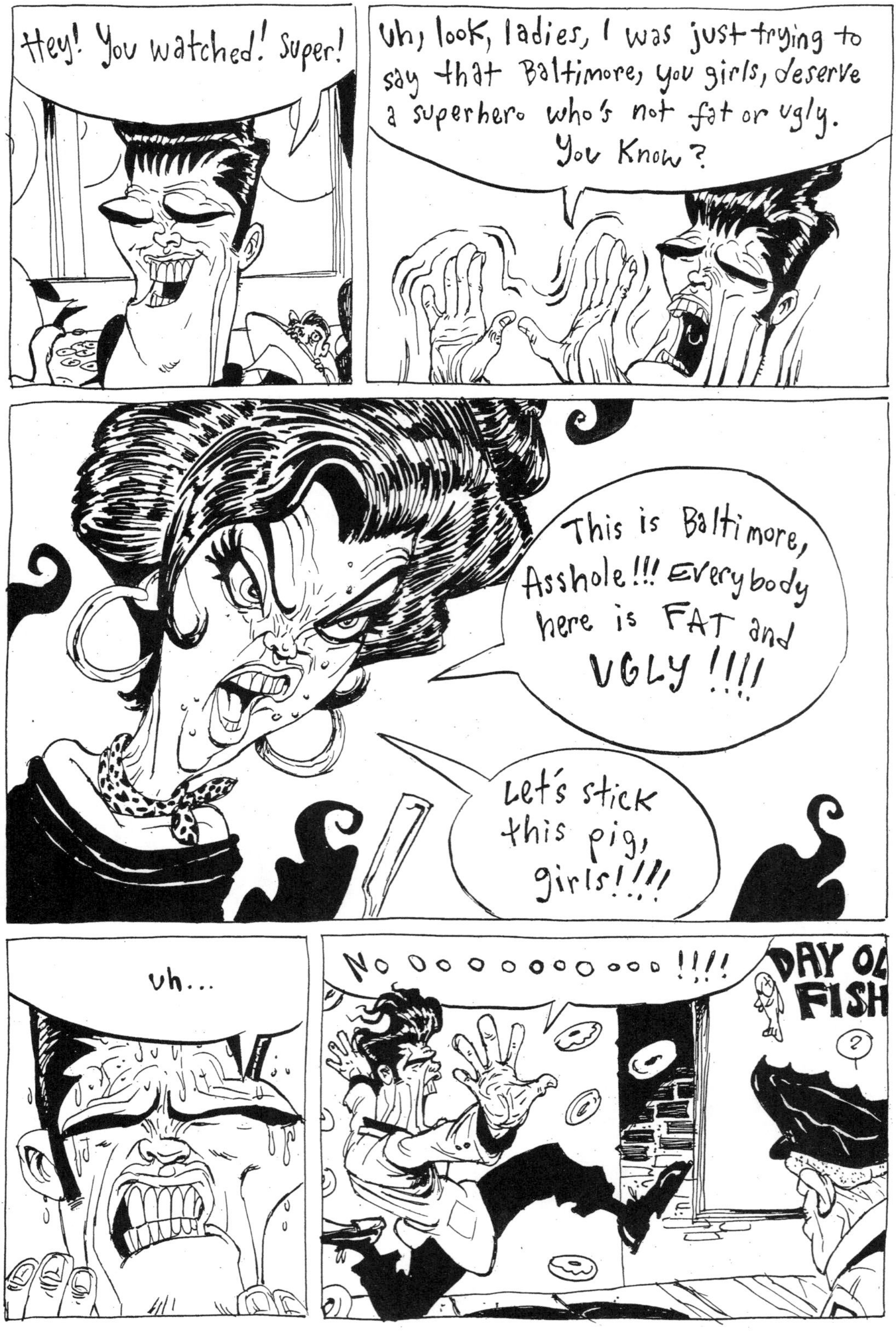
Hey! You watched! Super!
Uh, look, ladies, I was just trying to say that Baltimore, you girls, deserve a superhero who's not fat or ugly. You Know?
This is Baltimore, Asshole!!! Everybody here is FAT and UGLY!!!!
Let's stick this pig, girls!!!!
uh...
Nooooooooooo!!!!
DAY OL
FISH
?

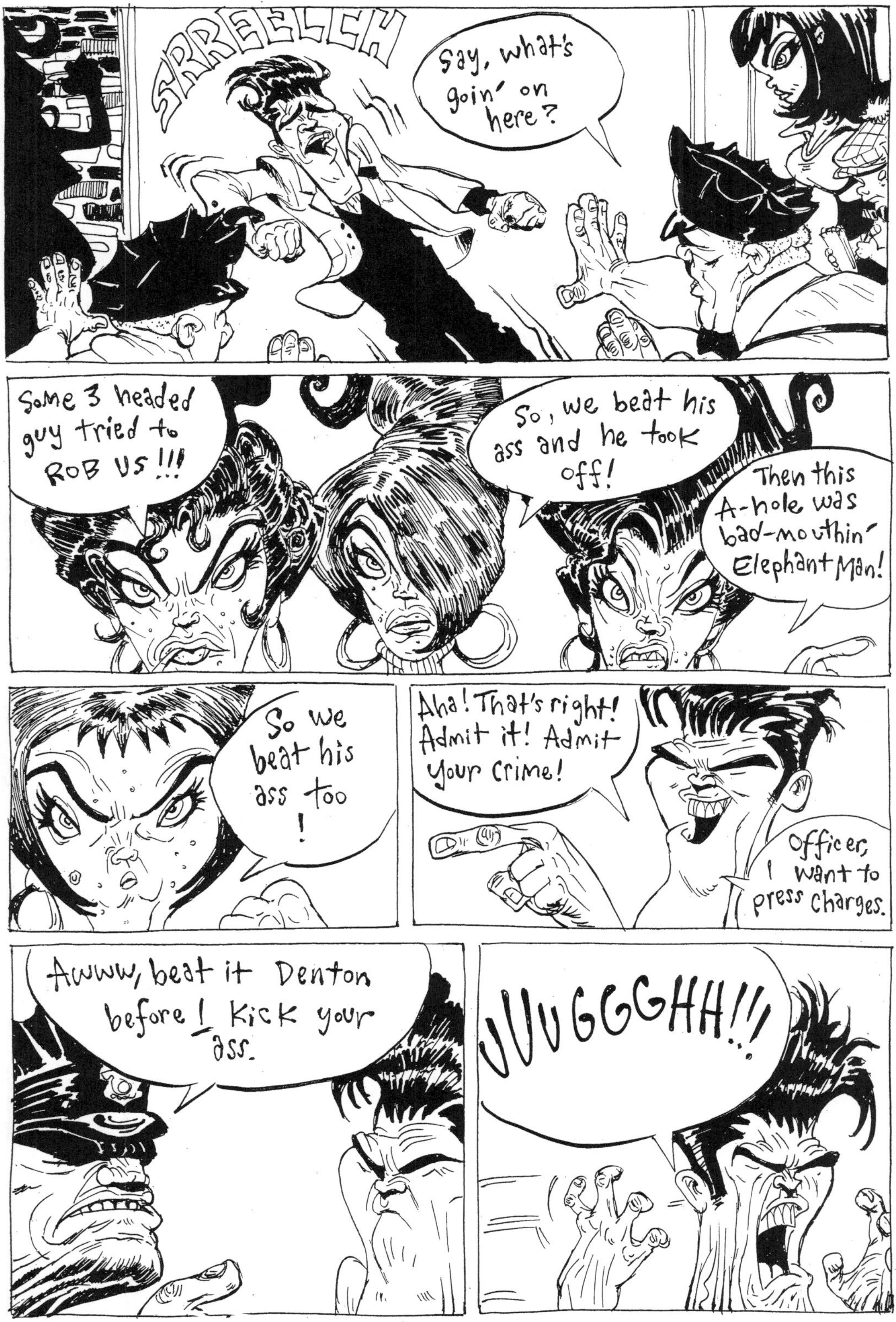
SRREELCH
Say, what's goin' on here?
Some 3 headed guy tried to ROB US!!!
So, we beat his ass and he took off!
Then this A-hole was bad-mouthin' Elephant Man!
So we beat his ass too !
Aha! That's right! Admit it! Admit your crime!
Officer, I want to press charges.
Awww, beat it Denton before I kick your ass.
UUUGGGHH!!!

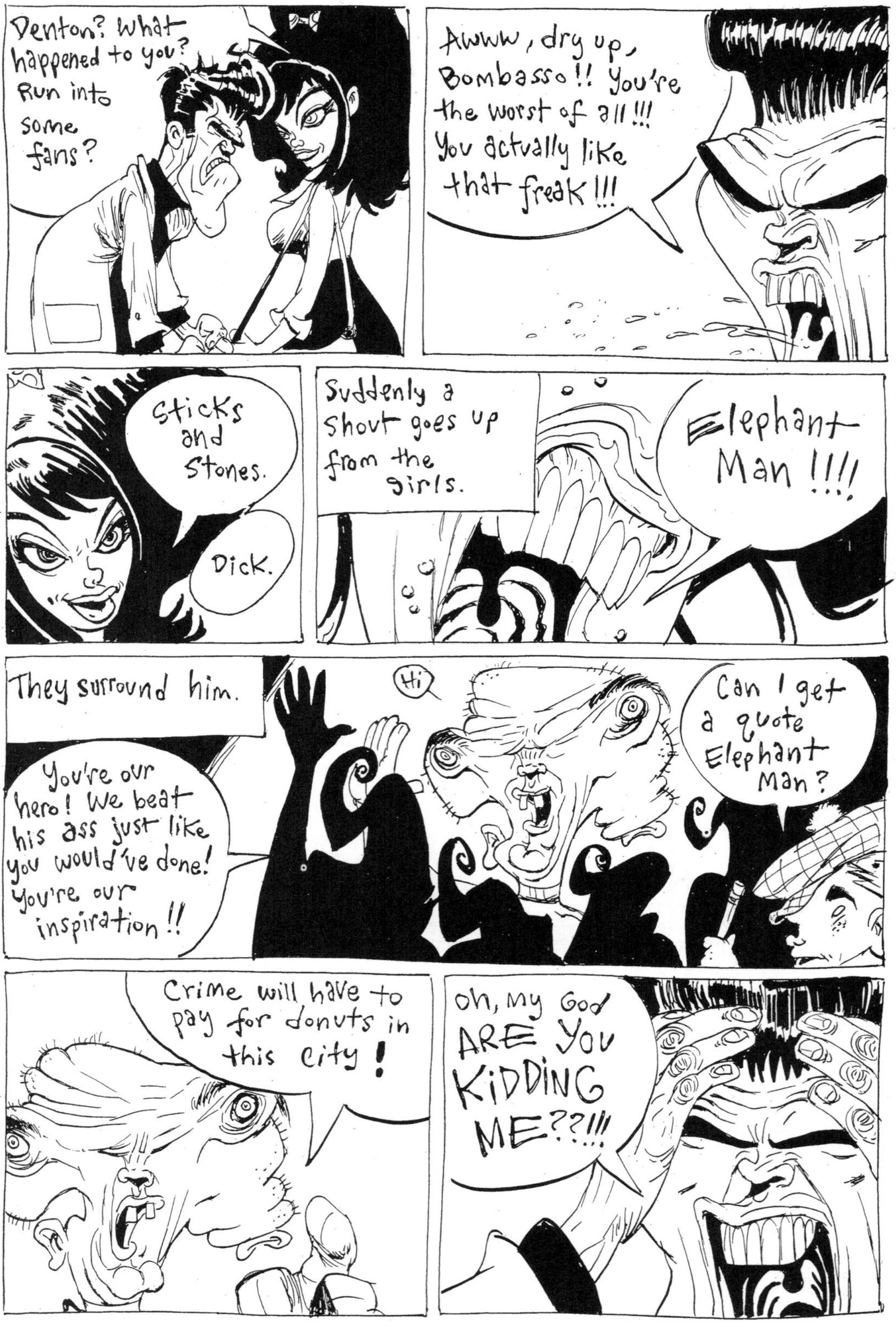

Denton? What happened to you? Run into some fans?
Awww, dry up, Bombasso!! You're the worst of all!!! You actually like that freak!!!
Sticks and Stones.
Dick.
Suddenly a shout goes up from the girls.
Elephant Man!!!!
They surround him.
Hi
Can I get a quote Elephant Man?
You're our hero! We beat his ass just like you would've done! You're our inspiration!!
Crime will have to pay for donuts in this city!
Oh, my God ARE YOU KIDDING ME??!!!

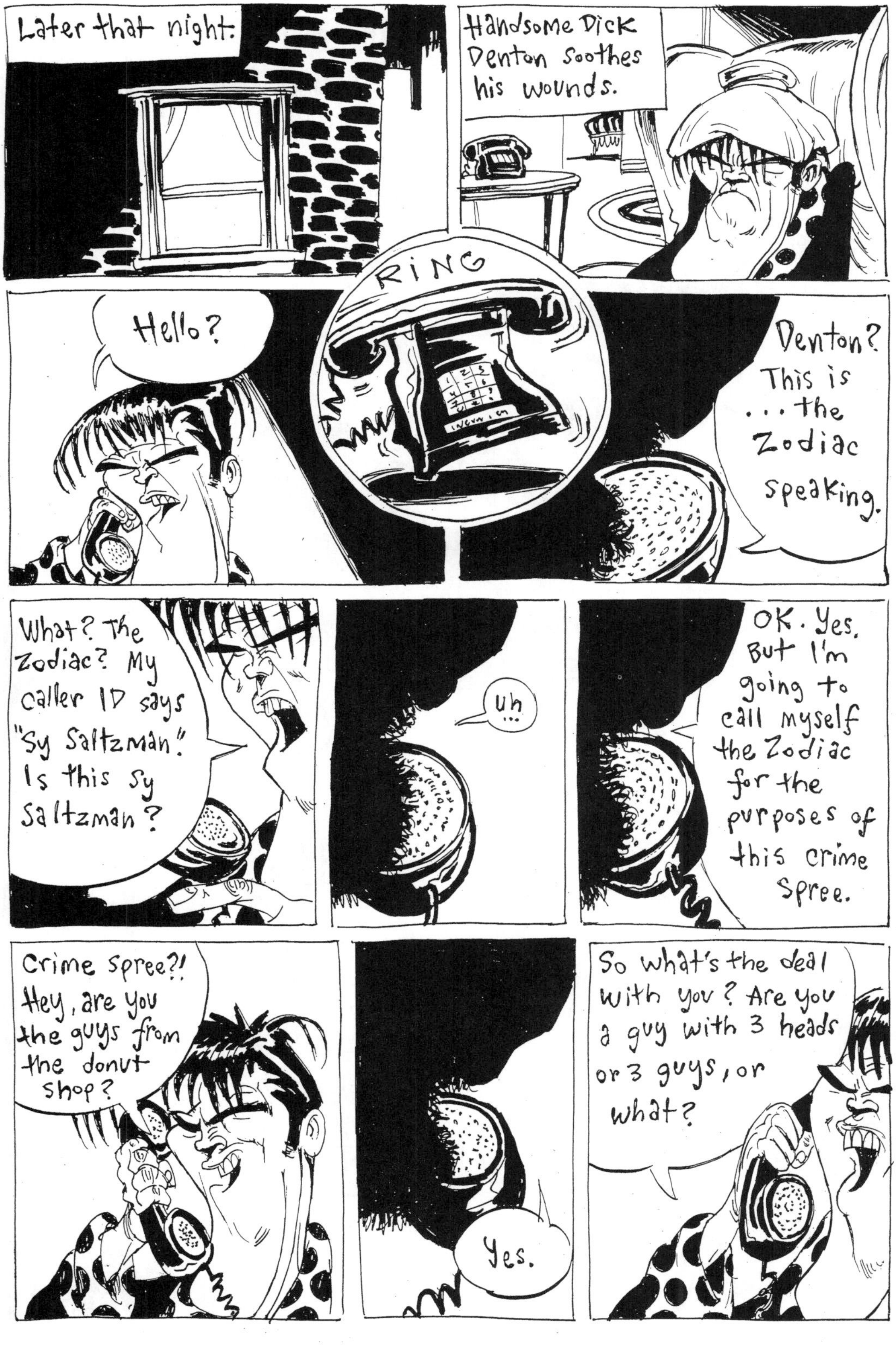
Later that night.
Handsome Dick Denton soothes his wounds.
RING
Hello?
Denton? This is . . . the Zodiac speaking.
What? The Zodiac? My caller ID says "Sy Saltzman." Is this Sy Saltzman?
Uh . . .
OK. Yes. But I'm going to call myself the Zodiac for the purposes of this crime spree.
Crime spree?! Hey, are you the guys from the donut shop?
Yes.
So what's the deal with you? Are you a guy with 3 heads or 3 guys, or what?

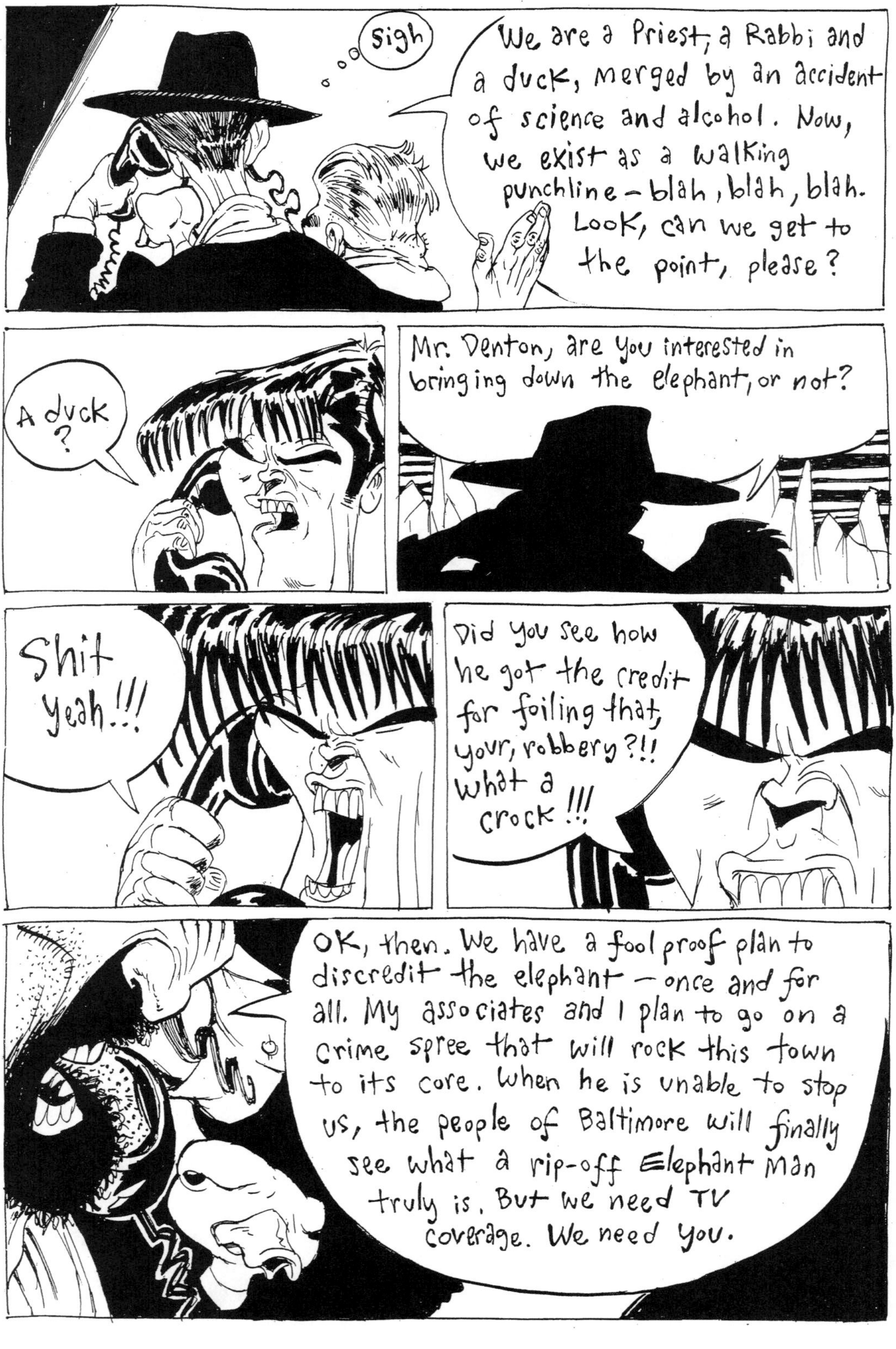
sigh
We are a Priest, a Rabbi and a duck, merged by an accident of science and alcohol. Now, we exist as a walking punchline - blah, blah, blah. Look, can we get to the point, please?
A duck?
Mr. Denton, are you interested in bringing down the elephant, or not?
Shit yeah!!!
Did you see how he got the credit for foiling that, your, robbery?!! What a crock!!!
OK, then. We have a fool proof plan to discredit the elephant - once and for all. My associates and I plan to go on a crime spree that will rock this town to its core. When he is unable to stop us, the people of Baltimore will finally see what a rip-off Elephant Man truly is. But we need TV coverage. We need you.

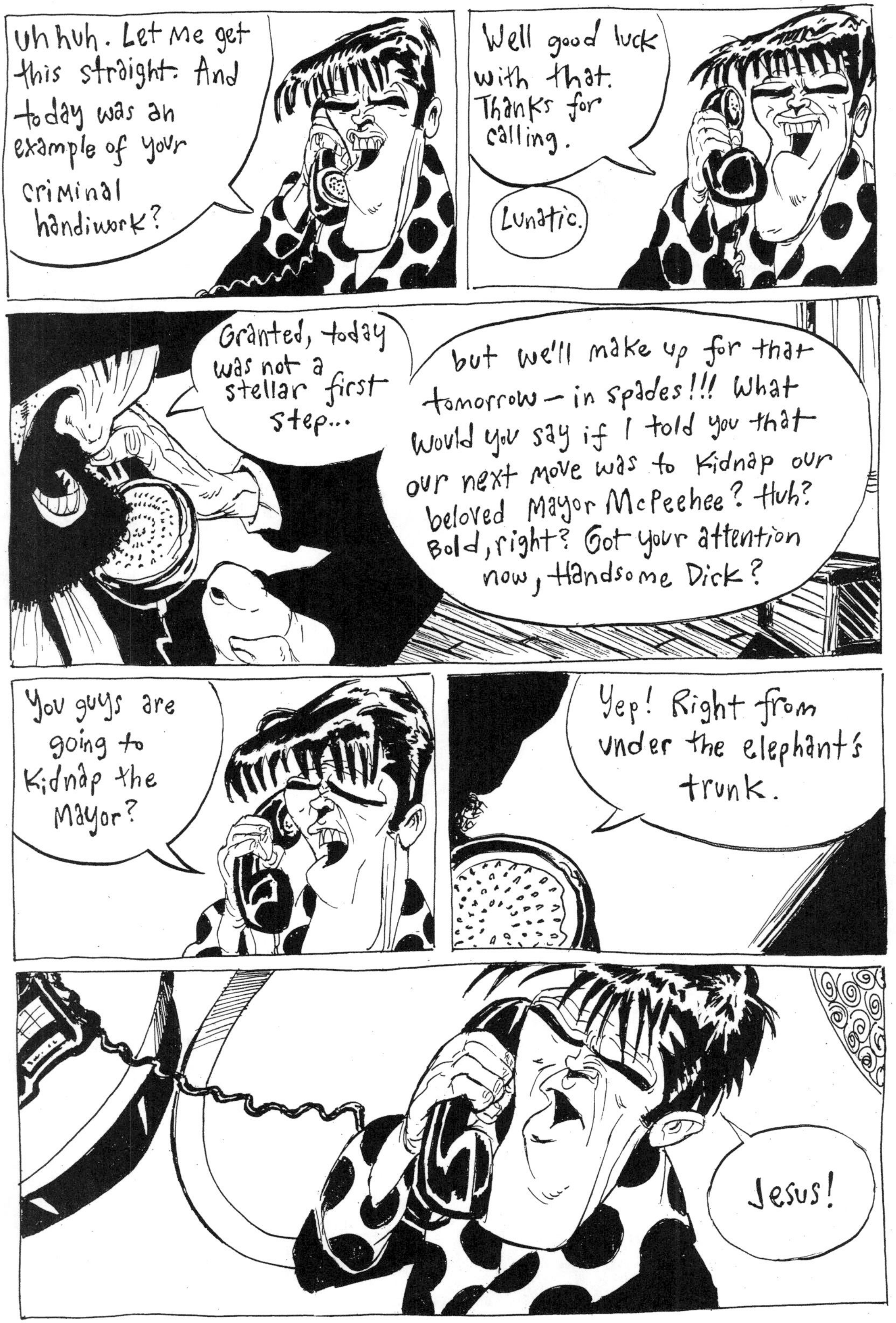
Uh huh. Let me get this straight. And today was an example of your criminal handiwork?
Well good luck with that. Thanks for calling.
Lunatic.
Granted, today was not a stellar first step...
but we'll make up for that tomorrow—in spades!!! What would you say if I told you that our next move was to kidnap our our beloved Mayor McPeehee? Huh? Bold, right? Got your attention now, Handsome Dick?
You guys are going to kidnap the Mayor?
Yep! Right from under the elephant's trunk.
Jesus!

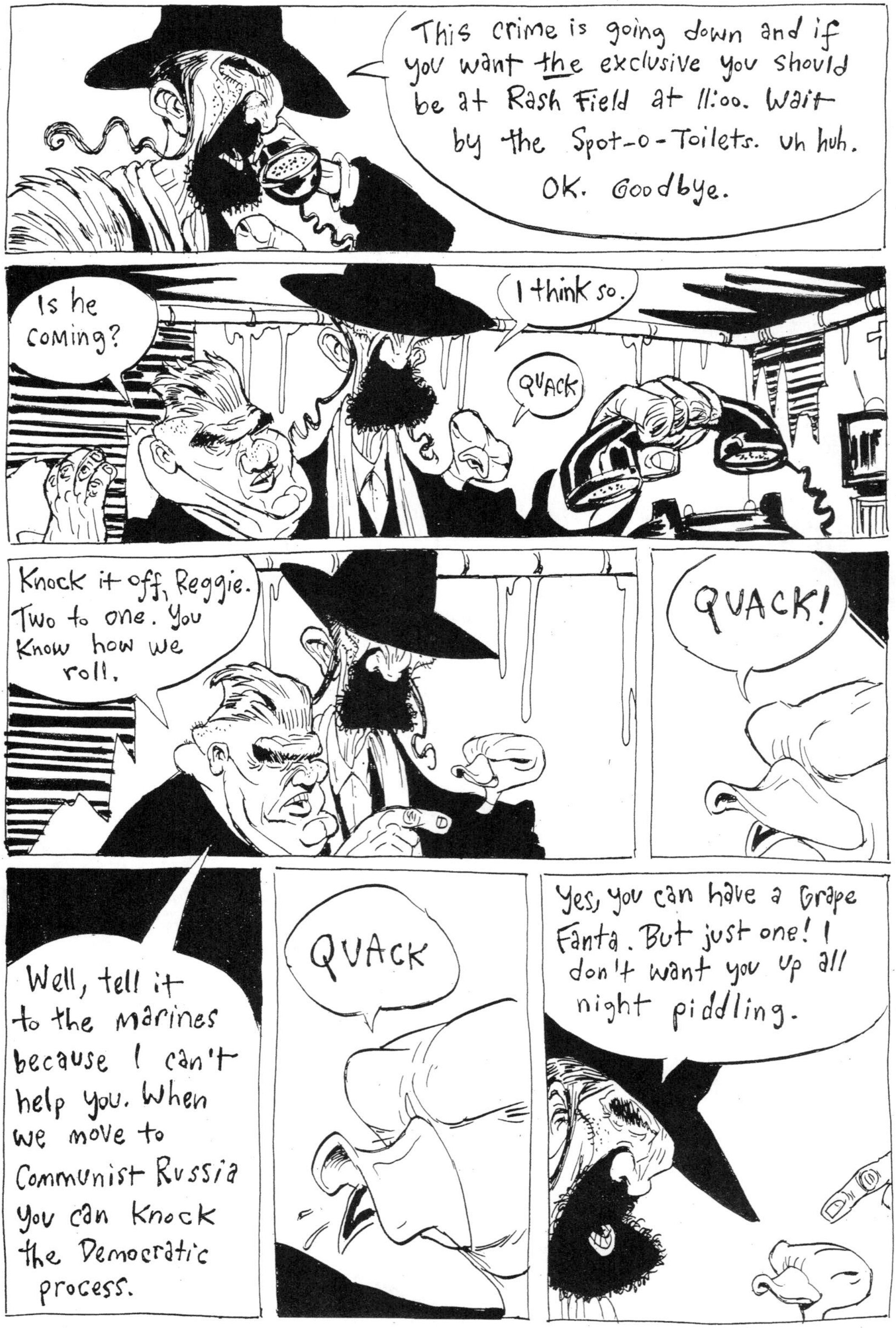
This crime is going down and if you want the exclusive you should be at Rash Field at 11:00. Wait by the Spot-o-Toilets. uh huh. OK. Goodbye.
Is he coming?
I think so.
QUACK
Knock it off, Reggie. Two to one. You Know how we roll.
QUACK!
Well, tell it to the marines because I can't help you. When we move to Communist Russia you can knock the Democratic process.
QUACK
Yes, you can have a Grape Fanta. But just one! I don't want you up all night piddling.

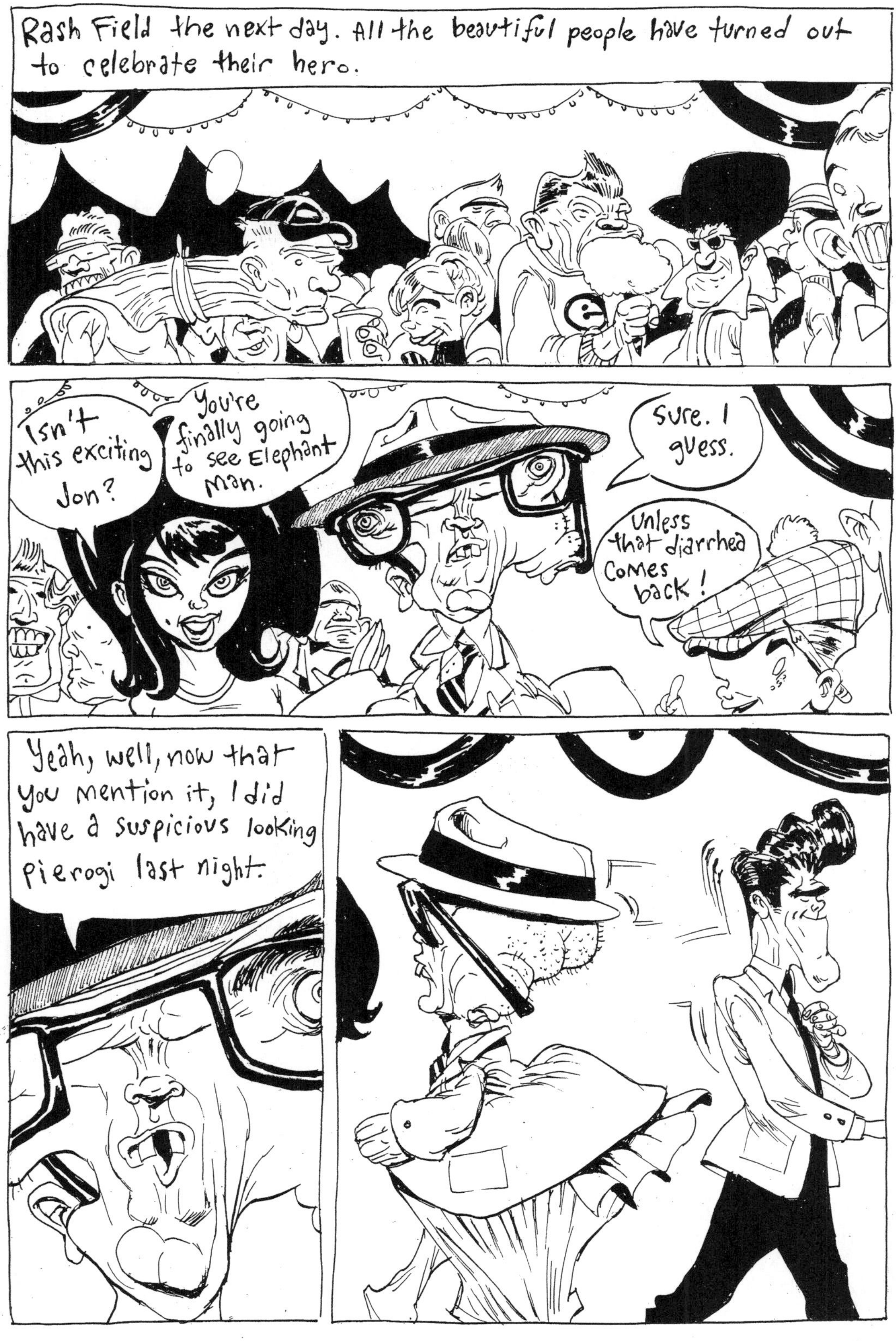
Rash Field the next day. All the beautiful people have turned out to celebrate their hero.
Isn't this exciting Jon?
You're finally going to see Elephant Man.
Sure. I guess.
Unless that diarrhea comes back!
Yeah, well, now that you mention it, I did have a suspicious looking pierogi last night.

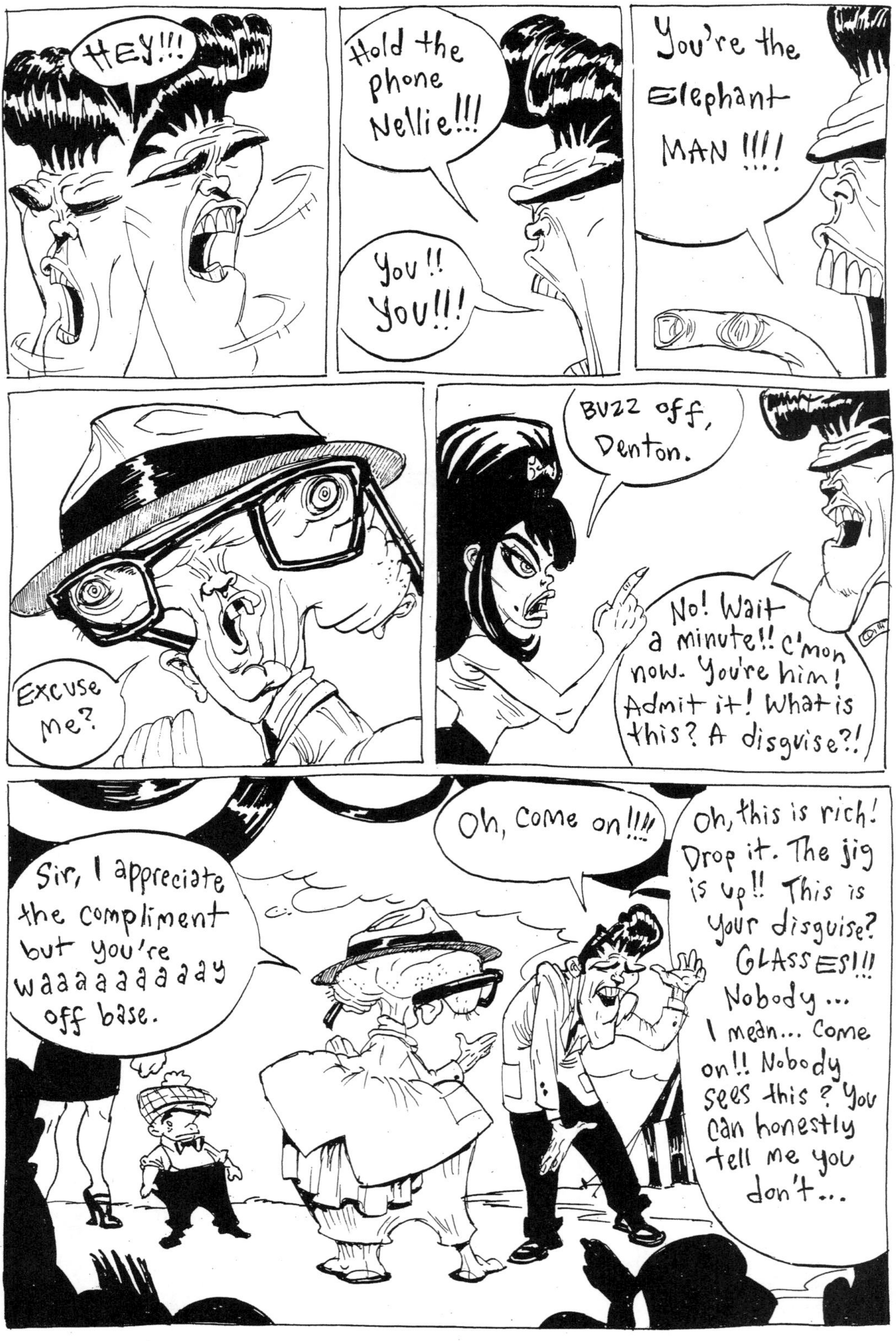
HEY!!!
Hold the phone Nellie!!!
You!! YOU!!!
You're the Elephant MAN!!!!
Excuse me?
BUZZ off, Denton.
No! Wait a minute!! C'mon now. You're him! Admit it! What is this? A disguise?!
Sir, I appreciate the compliment but you're waaaaaaaaay off base.
Oh, come on!!!!
Oh, this is rich! Drop it. The jig is up!! This is your disguise? GLASSES!!! Nobody... I mean... come on!! Nobody sees this? You can honestly tell me you don't...

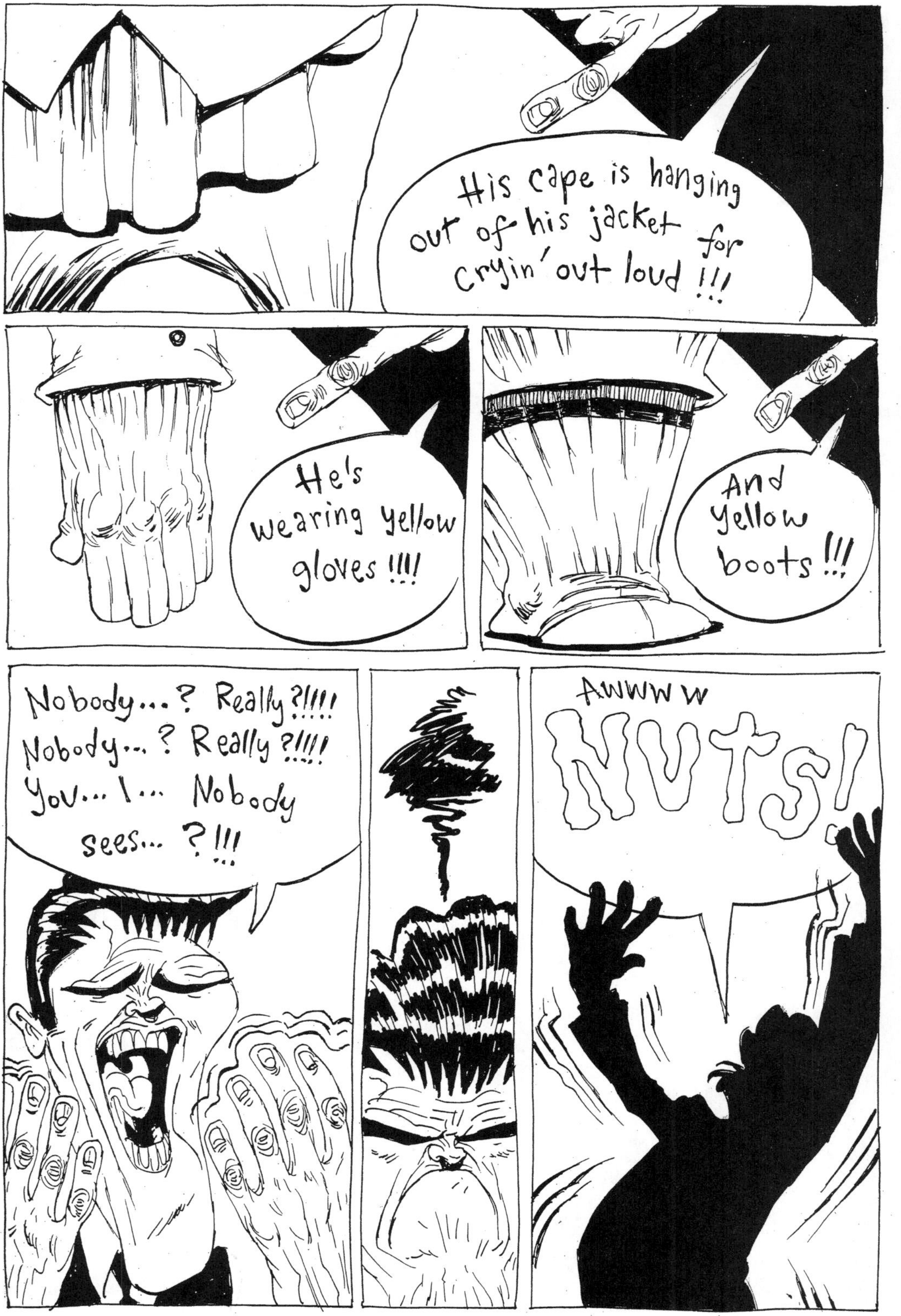

His cape is hanging out of his jacket for cryin' out loud !!!
He's wearing yellow gloves !!!!
And yellow boots !!!
Nobody...? Really?!!!! Nobody...? Really?!!!! You... I... Nobody sees... ?!!!
AWWWW NUTS!

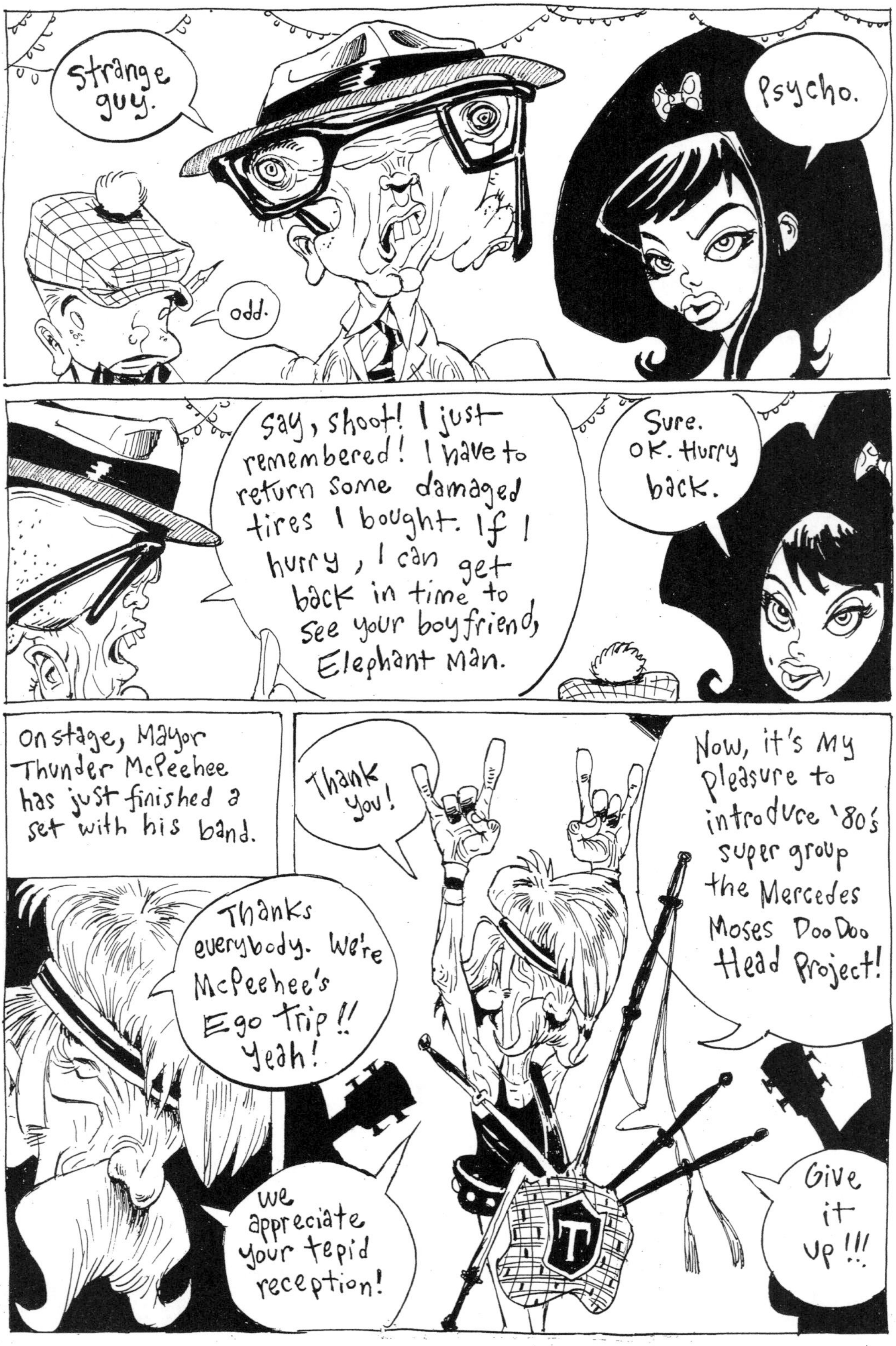

Strange guy.
odd.
Psycho.
Say, shoot! I just remembered! I have to return some damaged tires I bought. If I hurry, I can get back in time to see your boyfriend, Elephant Man.
Sure. OK. Hurry back.
Onstage, Mayor Thunder McPeehee has just finished a set with his band.
Thank you!
Now, it's my pleasure to introduce '80's super group the Mercedes Moses DooDoo Head Project!
Thanks everybody. We're McPeehee's Ego Trip!! Yeah!
We appreciate your tepid reception!
Give it up!!!

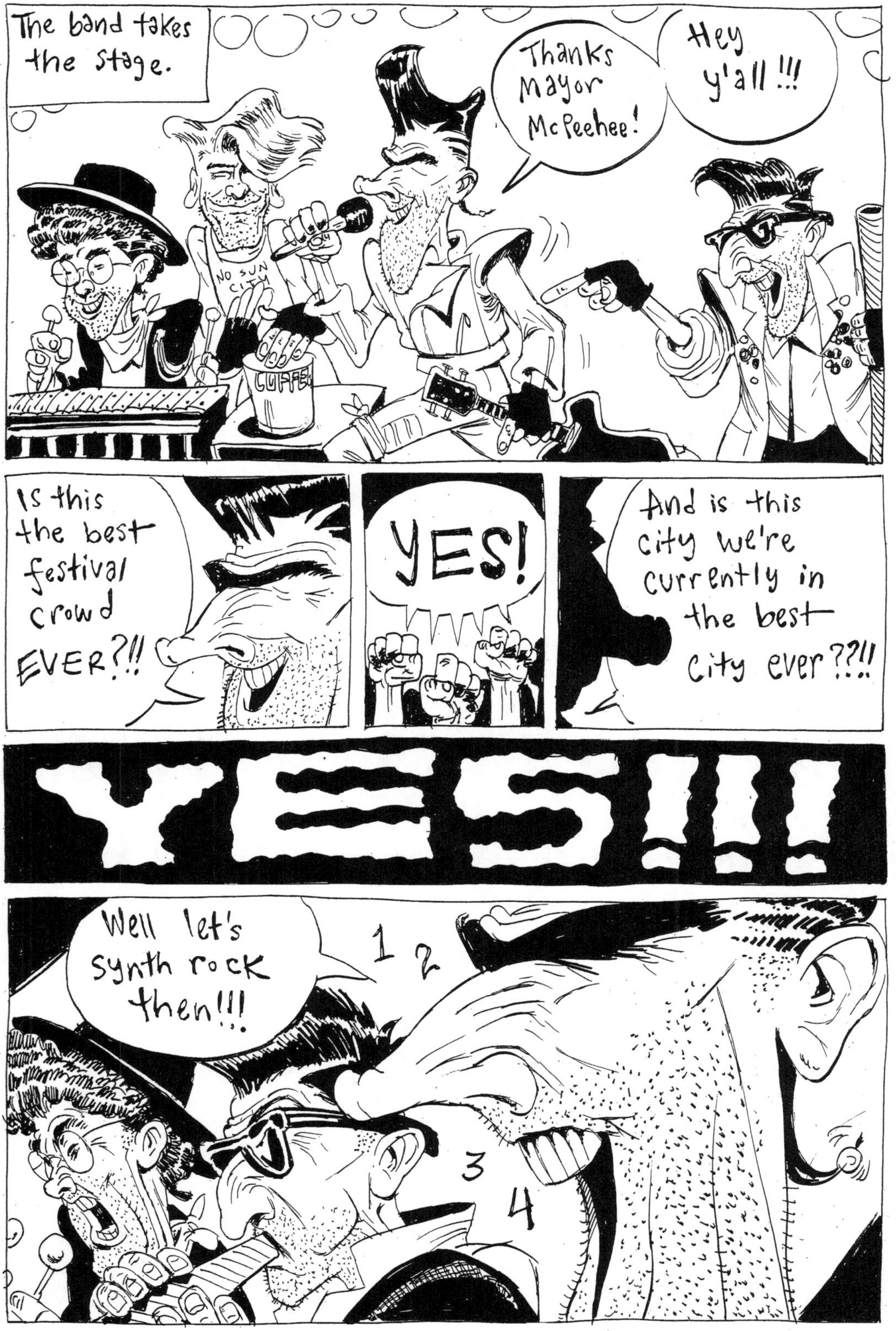

The band takes the stage.
Thanks Mayor McPeehee!
Hey y'all !!!
NO SUN CITY
Is this the best festival crowd EVER?!!
YES!
And is this city we're currently in the best city ever??!!
YES!!!
Well let's synth rock then!!!
1 2
3 4

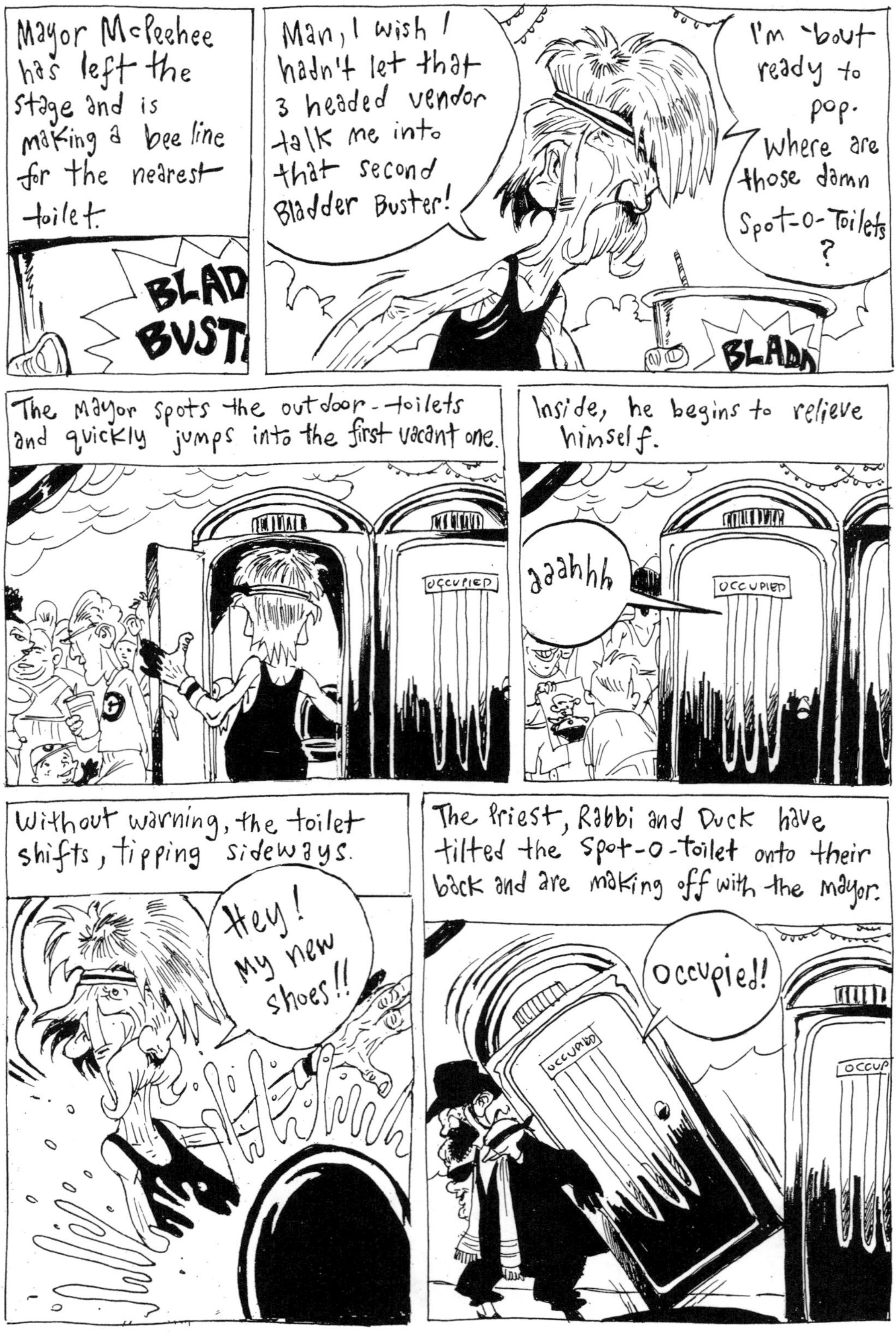
Mayor McGeehee has left the stage and is making a bee line for the nearest toilet.
BLAD BUST
Man, I wish I hadn't let that 3 headed vendor talk me into that second Bladder Buster!
I'm 'bout ready to pop. Where are those damn Spot-O-Toilets ?
BLADD
The Mayor spots the outdoor-toilets and quickly jumps into the first vacant one.
OCCUPIED
Inside, he begins to relieve himself.
aaahhh
OCCUPIED
Without warning, the toilet shifts, tipping sideways.
Hey! My new shoes!!
The Priest, Rabbi and Duck have tilted the Spot-O-toilet onto their back and are making off with the mayor.
Occupied!
OCCUPIED
OCCUP

AHAHAHA

OCCUPIED

Hey! Hey! Seriously! It's getting REALLY disgusting in here!!!!

Onstage, MMDDHP addresses the crowd.

Thanks! That was "I Got Skin (ALL OVER MY FACE)" from our classic '88 album, "Steps In Time"! But now, we'd like to dial it back and introduce the reason for the season, the big man himself—

ELEPHANT MAN !!!

From inside the Spot-o-Toilet in which he was changing identities, Elephant Man hears his name.

That's my cue.

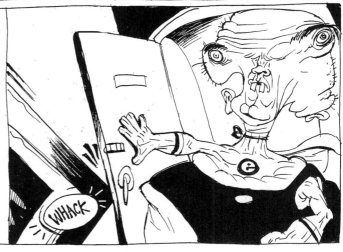

Having spent 25 minutes struggling to change into his costume (you thought the store room was small!), Elephant Man emerges from the portable toilet.

As he swings open the plastic door, he accidentally hits...

WHACK

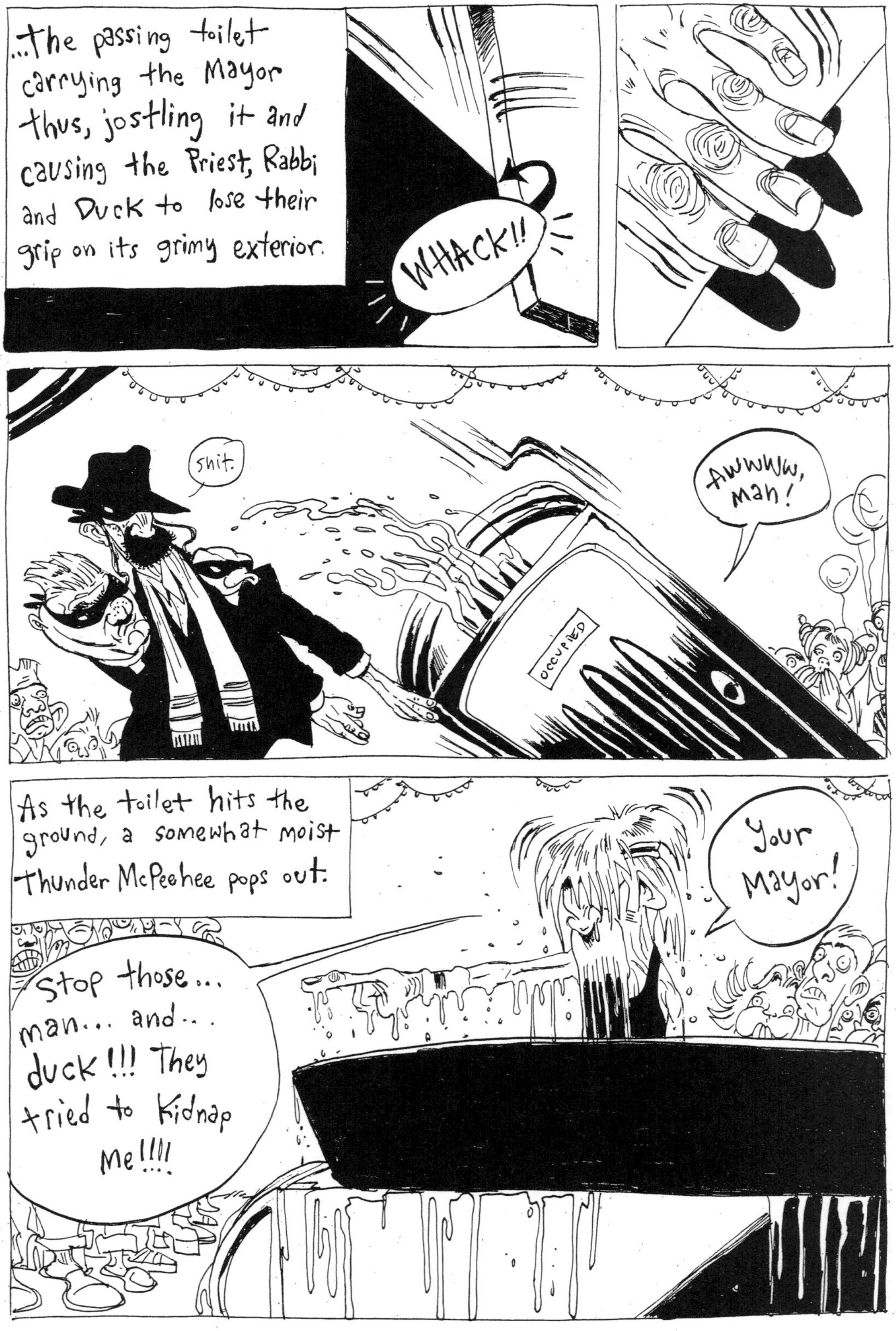

...The passing toilet carrying the Mayor thus, jostling it and causing the Priest, Rabbi and Duck to lose their grip on its grimy exterior.
WHACK!!
shit.
OCCUPIED
AWWWW, man!
As the toilet hits the ground, a somewhat moist Thunder McPeehee pops out.
Your Mayor!
Stop those... man... and... duck!!! They tried to Kidnap Me!!!!

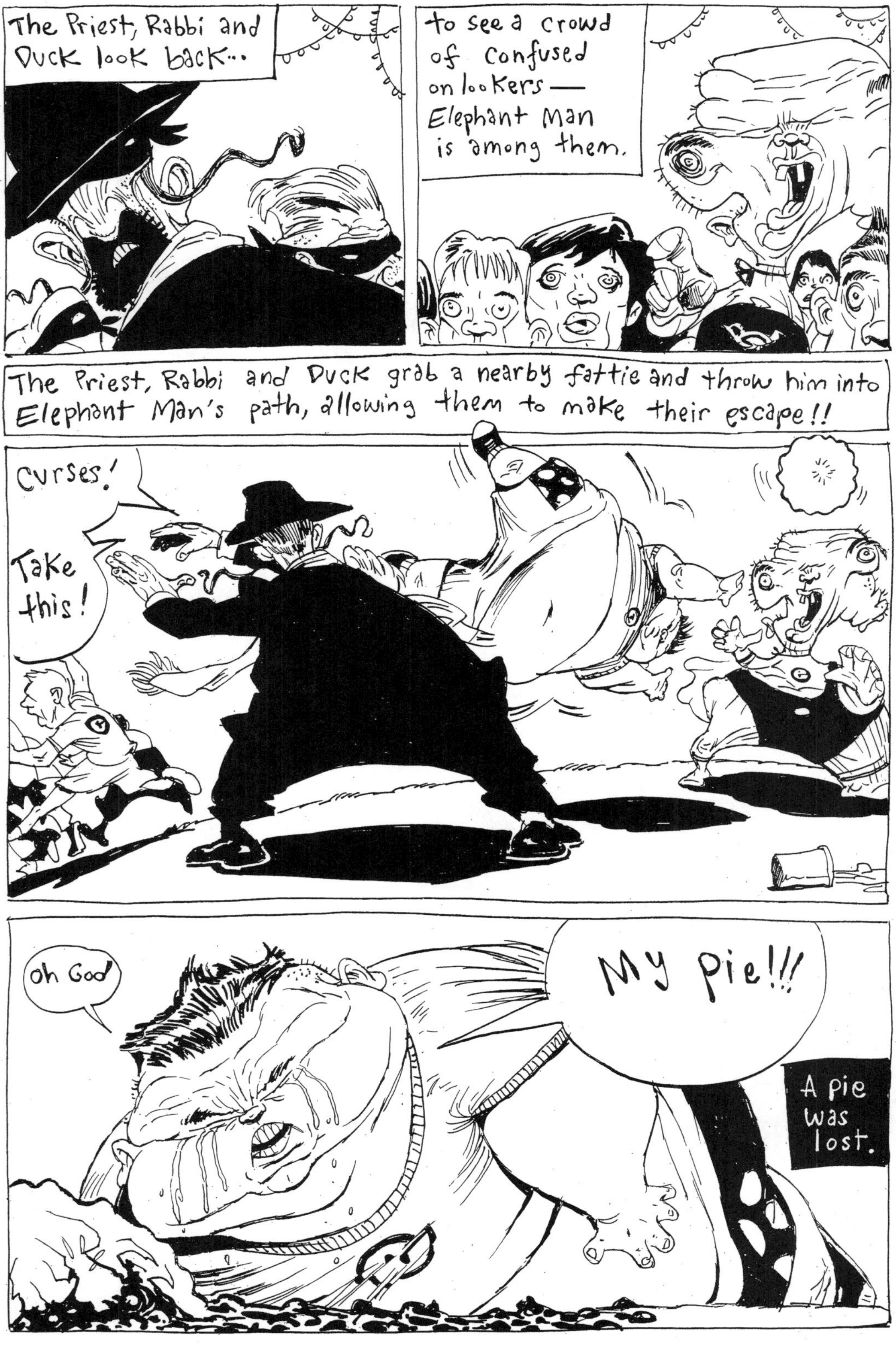

The Priest, Rabbi and Duck look back...
to see a crowd of confused onlookers — Elephant Man is among them.
The Priest, Rabbi and Duck grab a nearby fattie and throw him into Elephant Man's path, allowing them to make their escape!!
Curses!
Take this!
oh God
My pie!!!
A pie was lost.

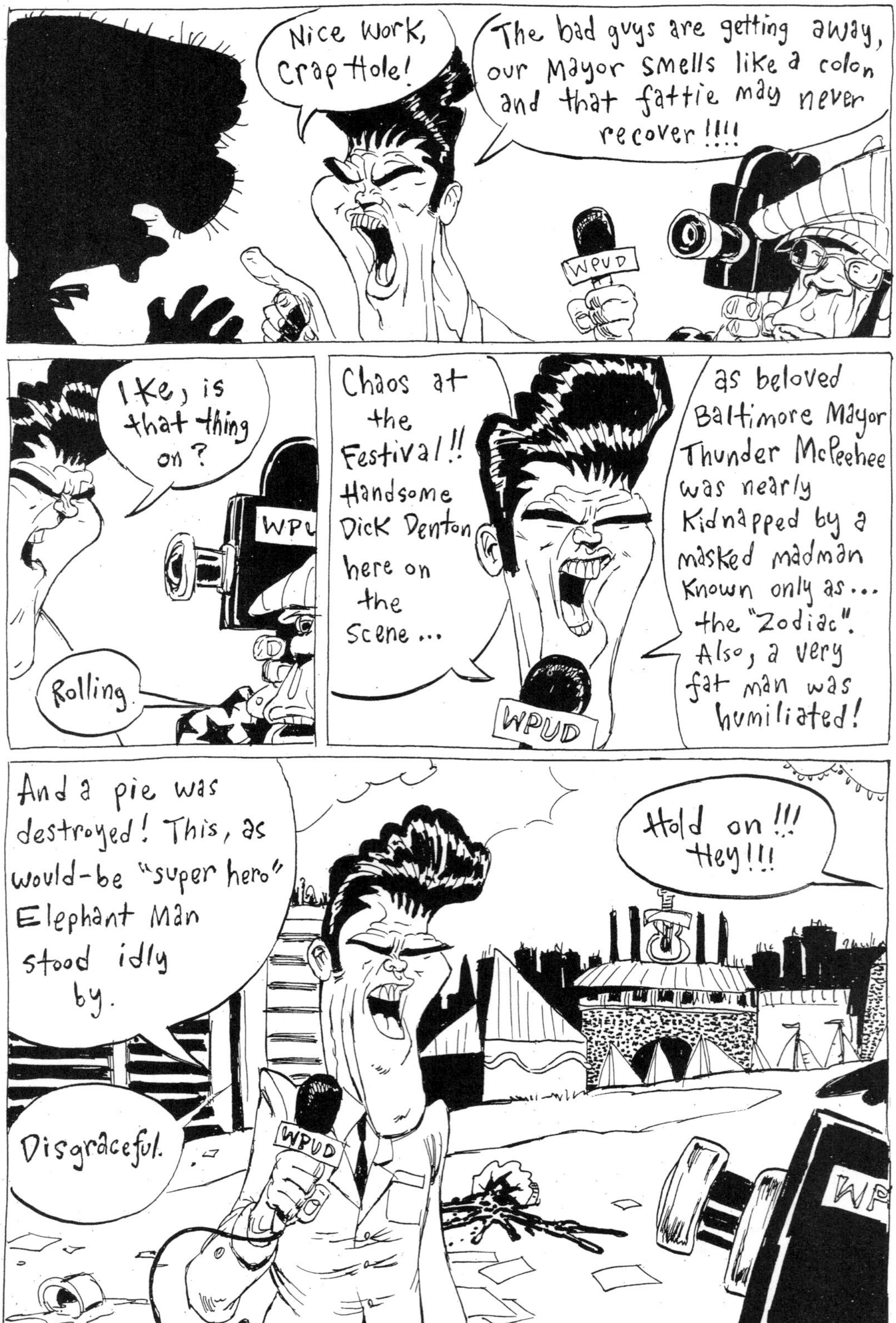
Nice Work, Crap Hole!
The bad guys are getting away, our Mayor smells like a colon and that fattie may never recover!!!!
WPUD
Ike, is that thing on?
WPU
Rolling.
Chaos at the Festival!! Handsome Dick Denton here on the scene...
as beloved Baltimore Mayor Thunder McPeehee was nearly Kidnapped by a masked madman Known only as... the "Zodiac". Also, a very fat man was humiliated!
WPUD
And a pie was destroyed! This, as would-be "super hero" Elephant Man stood idly by.
Hold on!!! Hey!!!
Disgraceful.
WPUD
WP

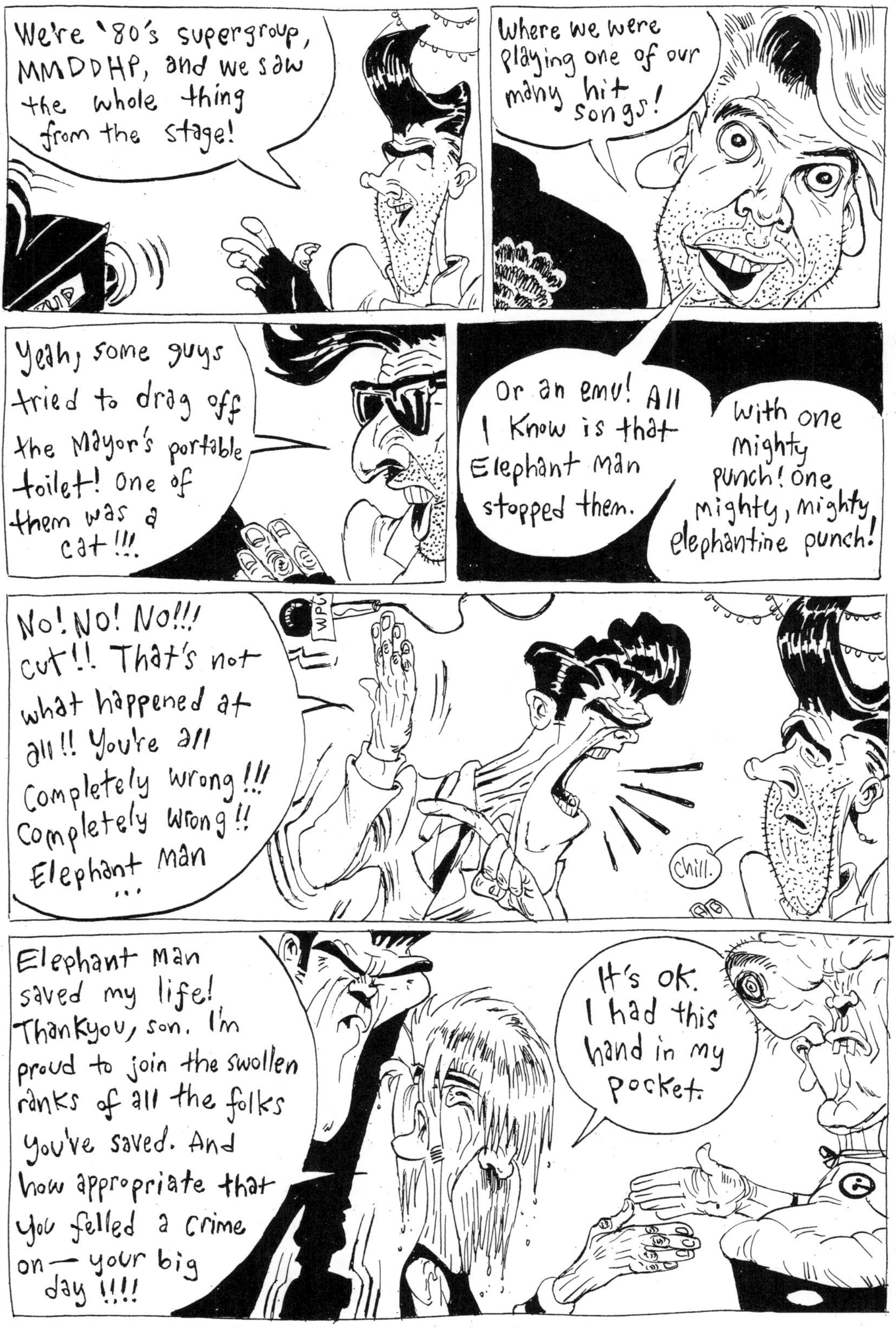
We're '80's supergroup, MMDDHP, and we saw the whole thing from the stage!
Where we were playing one of our many hit songs!
Yeah, some guys tried to drag off the Mayor's portable toilet! One of them was a cat!!!
Or an emu! All I know is that Elephant Man stopped them.
With one mighty punch! One mighty, mighty elephantine punch!
No! No! No!!! Cut!! That's not what happened at all!! You're all completely wrong!!! Completely wrong!! Elephant Man ...
WPU
Chill.
Elephant Man saved my life! Thankyou, son. I'm proud to join the swollen ranks of all the folks you've saved. And how appropriate that you felled a crime on— your big day!!!!
It's OK. I had this hand in my pocket.

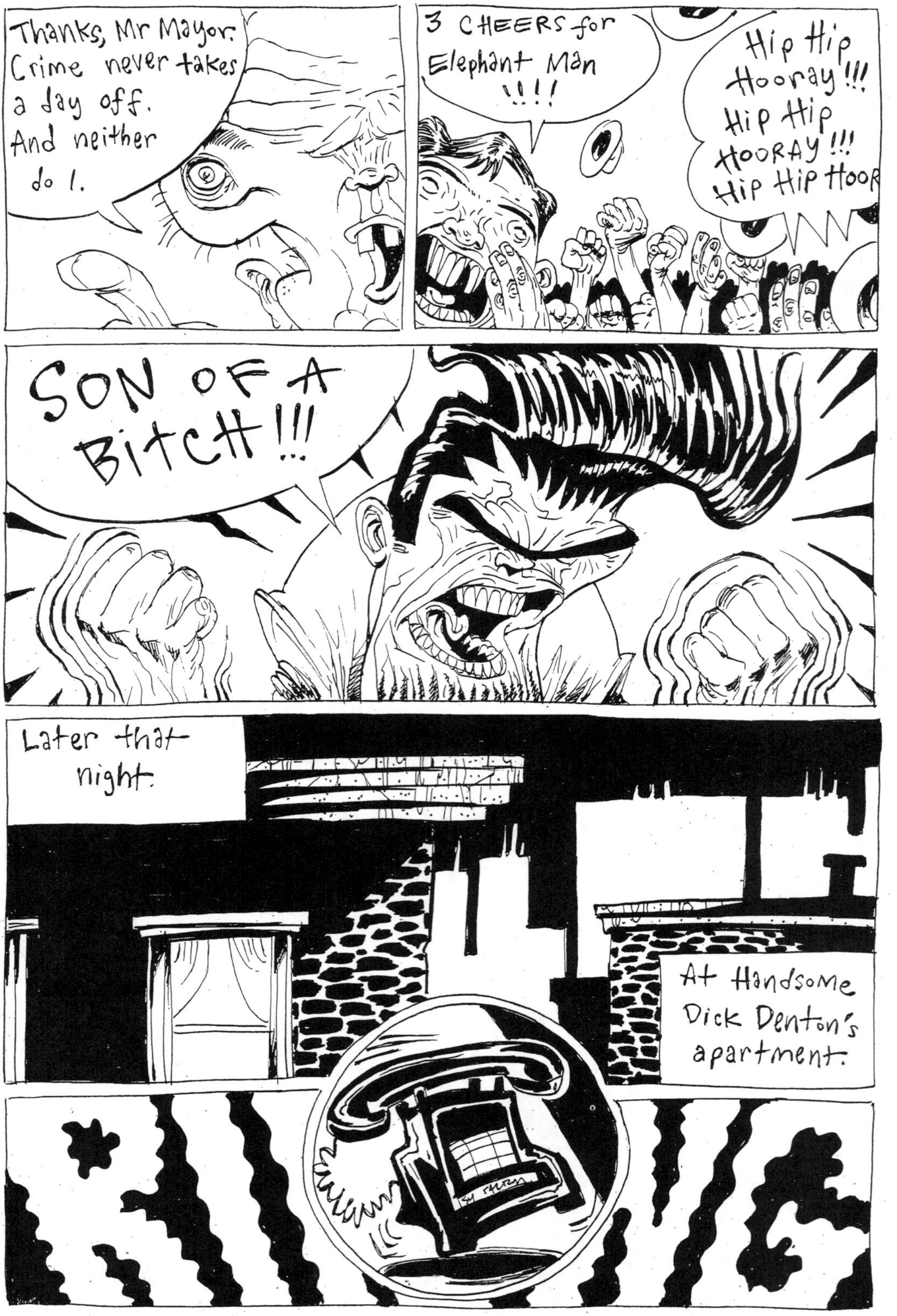
Thanks, Mr Mayor. Crime never takes a day off. And neither do I.
3 CHEERS for Elephant Man !!!!
Hip Hip Hooray!!! Hip Hip HOORAY!!! Hip Hip Hoor
SON OF A BITCH!!!
Later that night.
At Handsome Dick Denton's apartment.

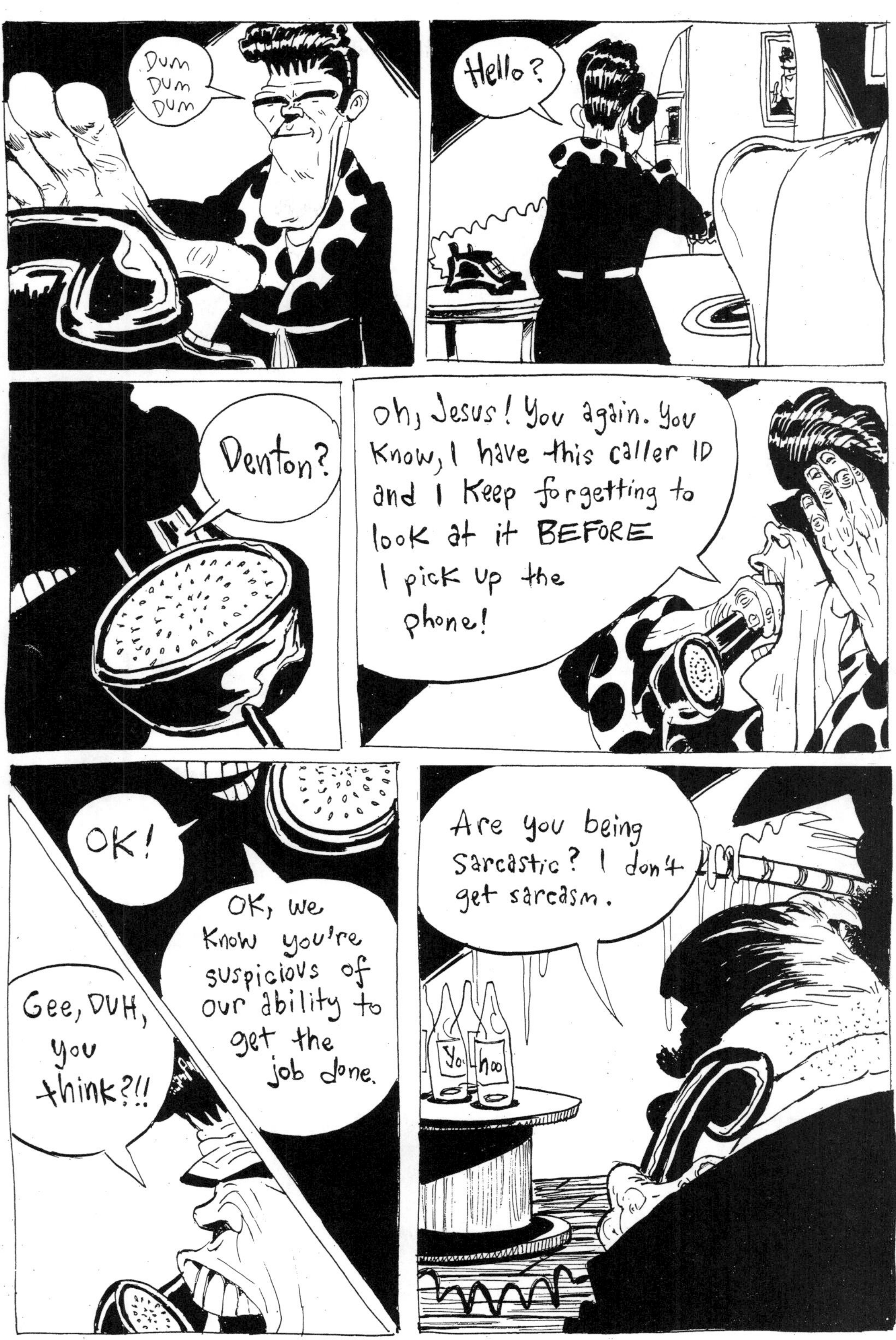

Dum Dum Dum
Hello?
Denton?
Oh, Jesus! You again. You know, I have this caller ID and I keep forgetting to look at it BEFORE I pick up the phone!
OK!
OK, we know you're suspicious of our ability to get the job done.
Gee, DUH, you think?!!
Are you being sarcastic? I don't get sarcasm.
Yoo
hoo

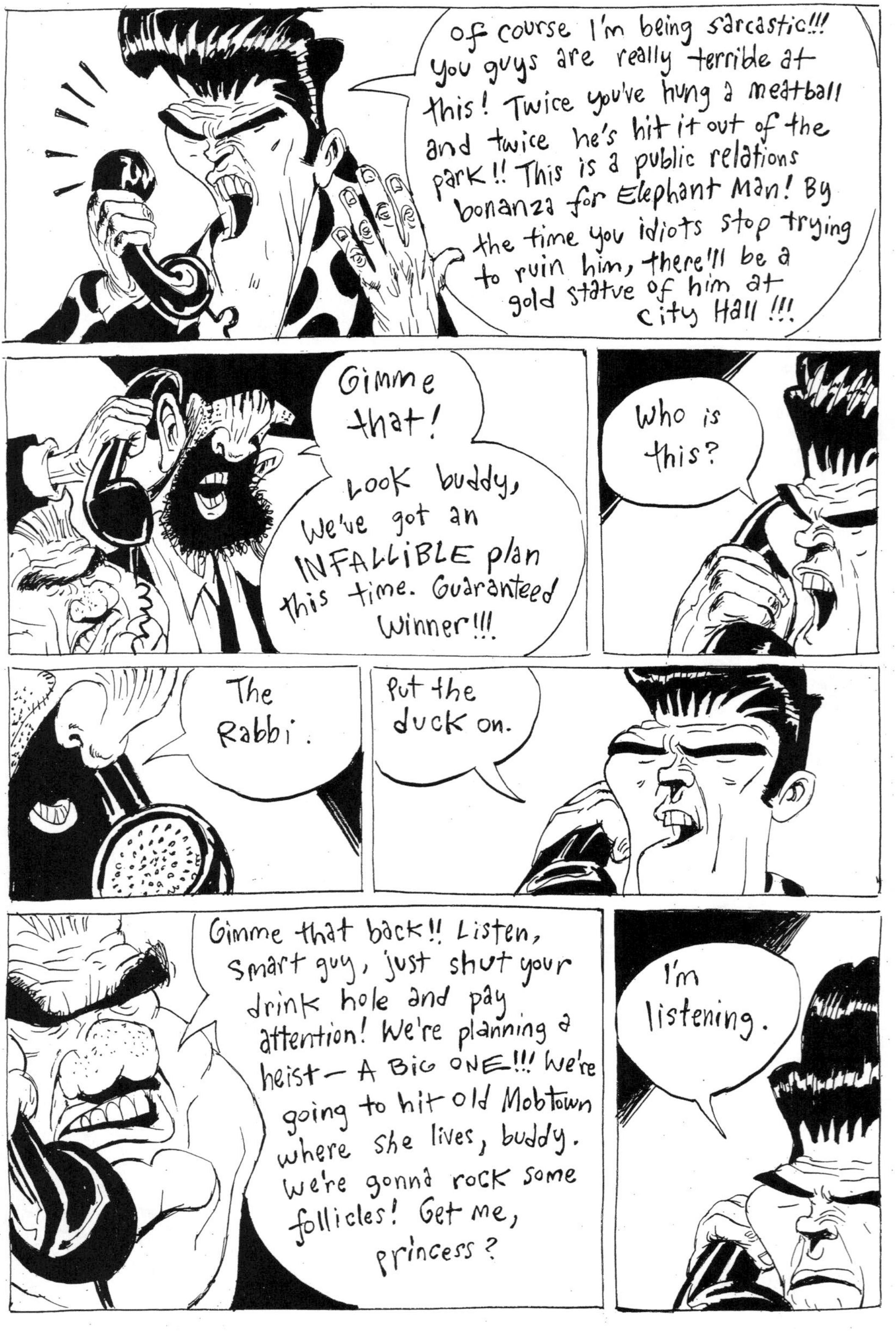
Of course I'm being sarcastic!!! You guys are really terrible at this! Twice you've hung a meatball and twice he's hit it out of the park!! This is a public relations bonanza for Elephant Man! By the time you idiots stop trying to ruin him, there'll be a gold statue of him at City Hall!!!
Gimme that!
Look buddy, We've got an INFALLIBLE plan this time. Guaranteed Winner!!!
Who is this?
The Rabbi.
Put the duck on.
Gimme that back!! Listen, smart guy, just shut your drink hole and pay attention! We're planning a heist— A BIG ONE!!! We're going to hit old Mobtown where she lives, buddy. We're gonna rock some follicles! Get me, princess?
I'm listening.

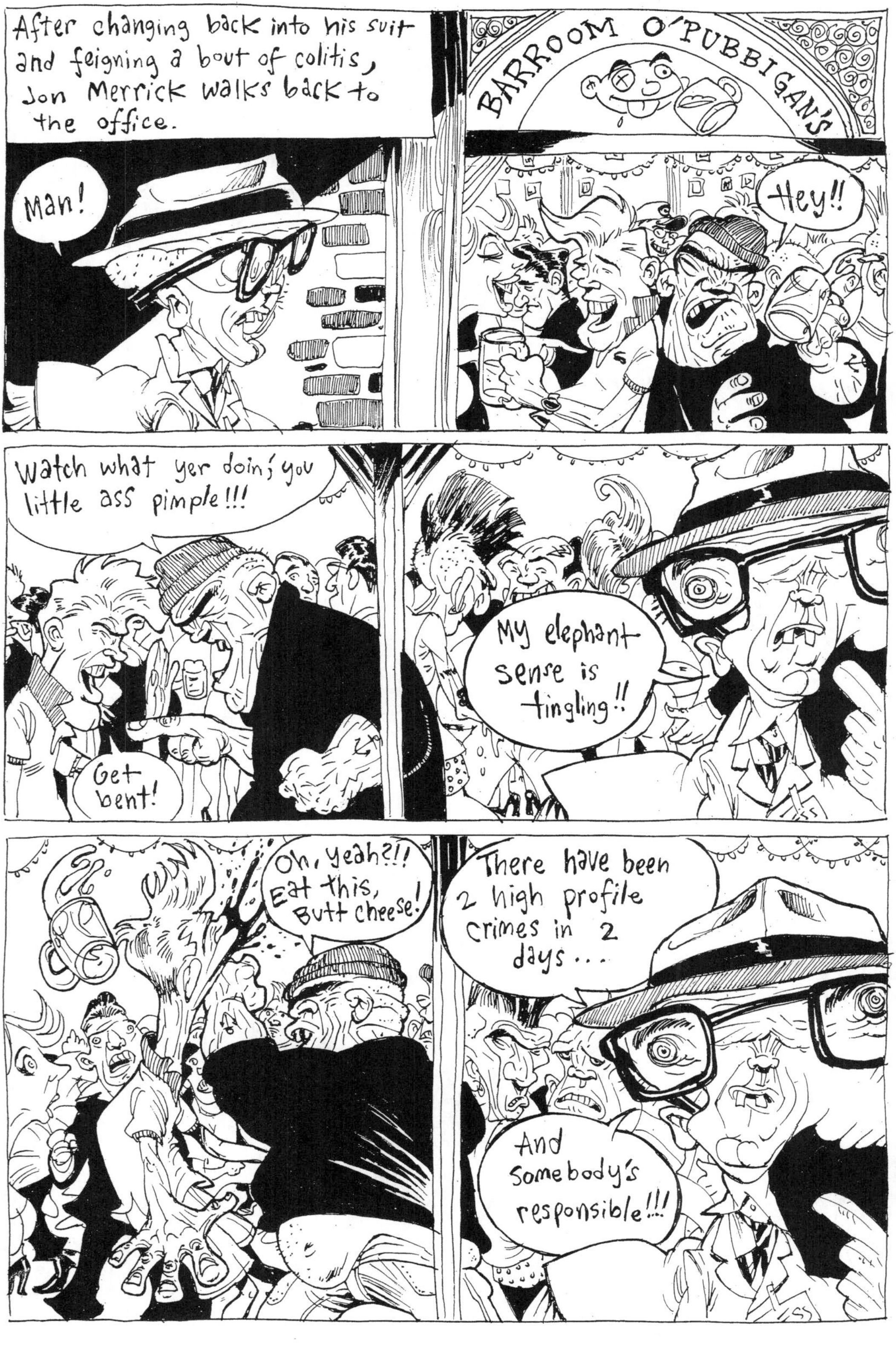
After changing back into his suit and feigning a bout of colitis, Jon Merrick walks back to the office.
BARROOM O'PUBBIGAN'S
Man!
Hey!!
Watch what yer doin', you little ass pimple!!!
Get bent!
My elephant sense is tingling!!
Oh, yeah?!! Eat this, Butt cheese!
There have been 2 high profile crimes in 2 days...
And somebody's responsible!!!

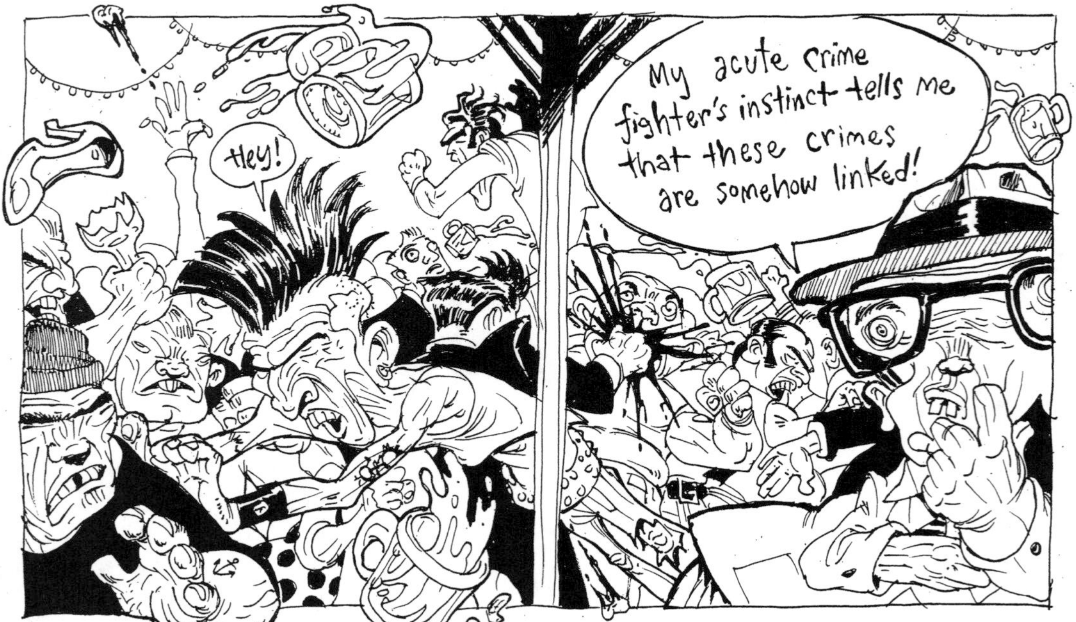
Hey!
My acute crime fighter's instinct tells me that these crimes are somehow linked!

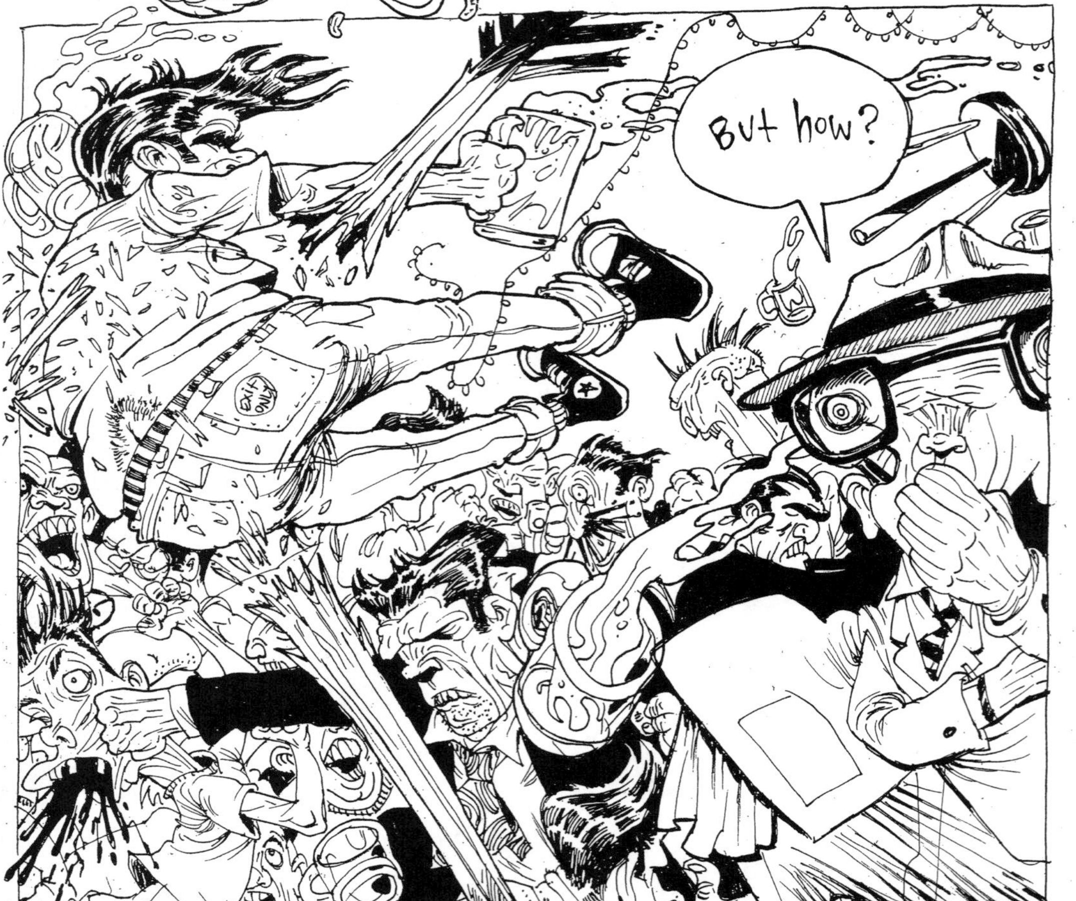
But how?

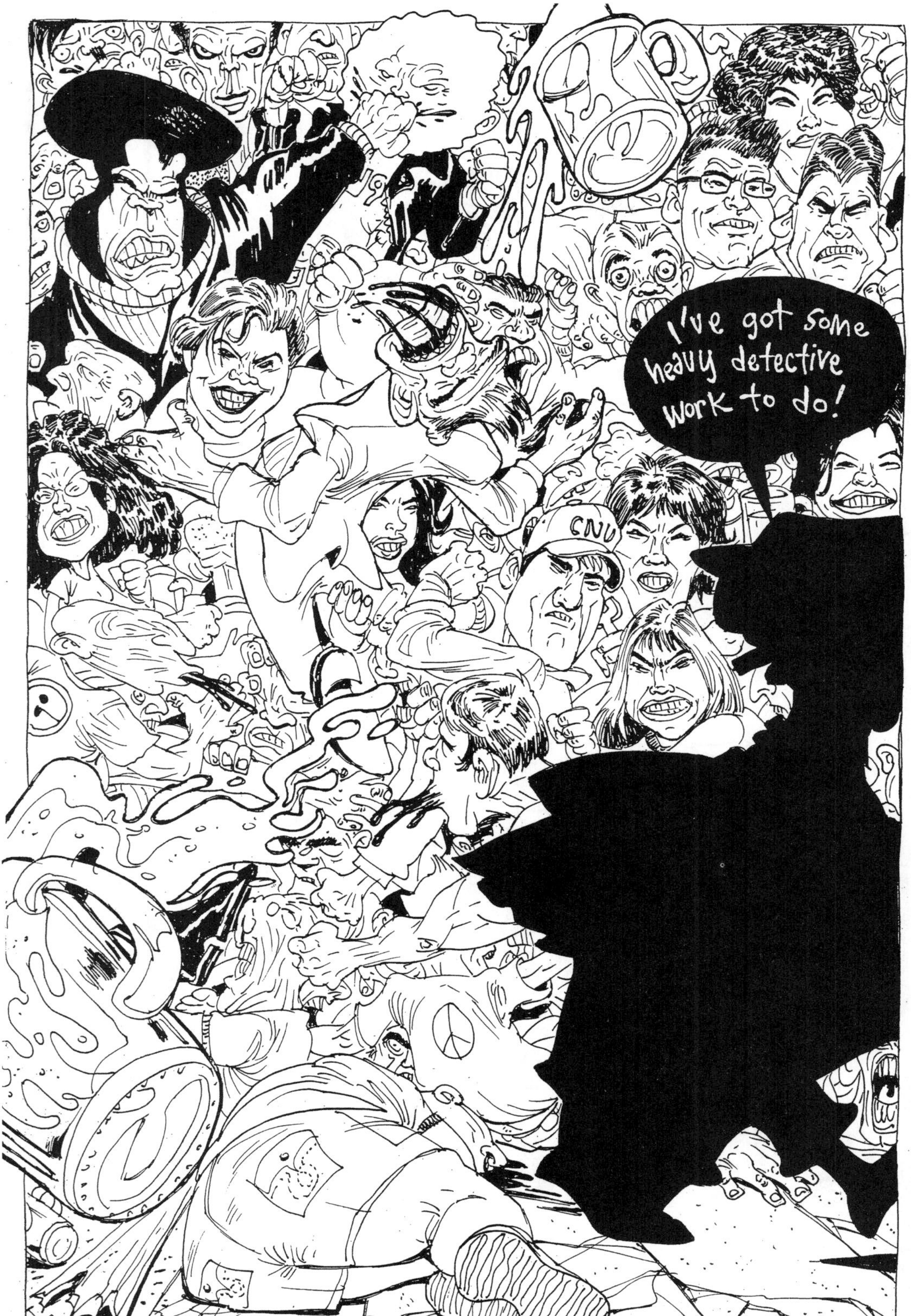
I've got some heavy detective work to do!
CNU

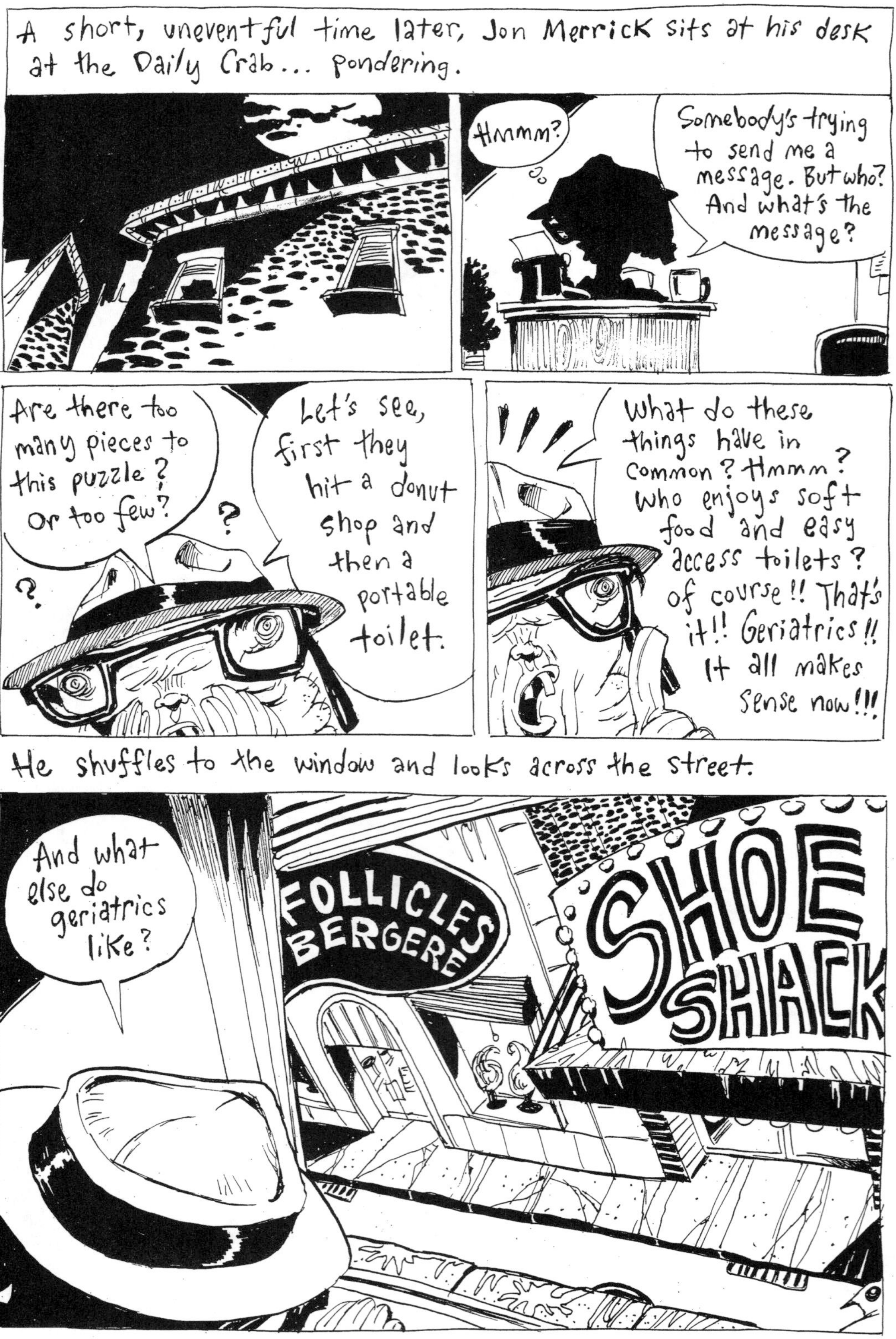
A short, uneventful time later, Jon Merrick sits at his desk at the Daily Crab... pondering.
Hmmm?
Somebody's trying to send me a message. But who? And what's the message?
Are there too many pieces to this puzzle? Or too few?
?
?
Let's see, first they hit a donut shop and then a portable toilet.
What do these things have in common? Hmmm? Who enjoys soft food and easy access toilets? Of course!! That's it!! Geriatrics!! It all makes sense now!!!
He shuffles to the window and looks across the street.
And what else do geriatrics like?
FOLLICLES BERGERE
SHOE SHACK

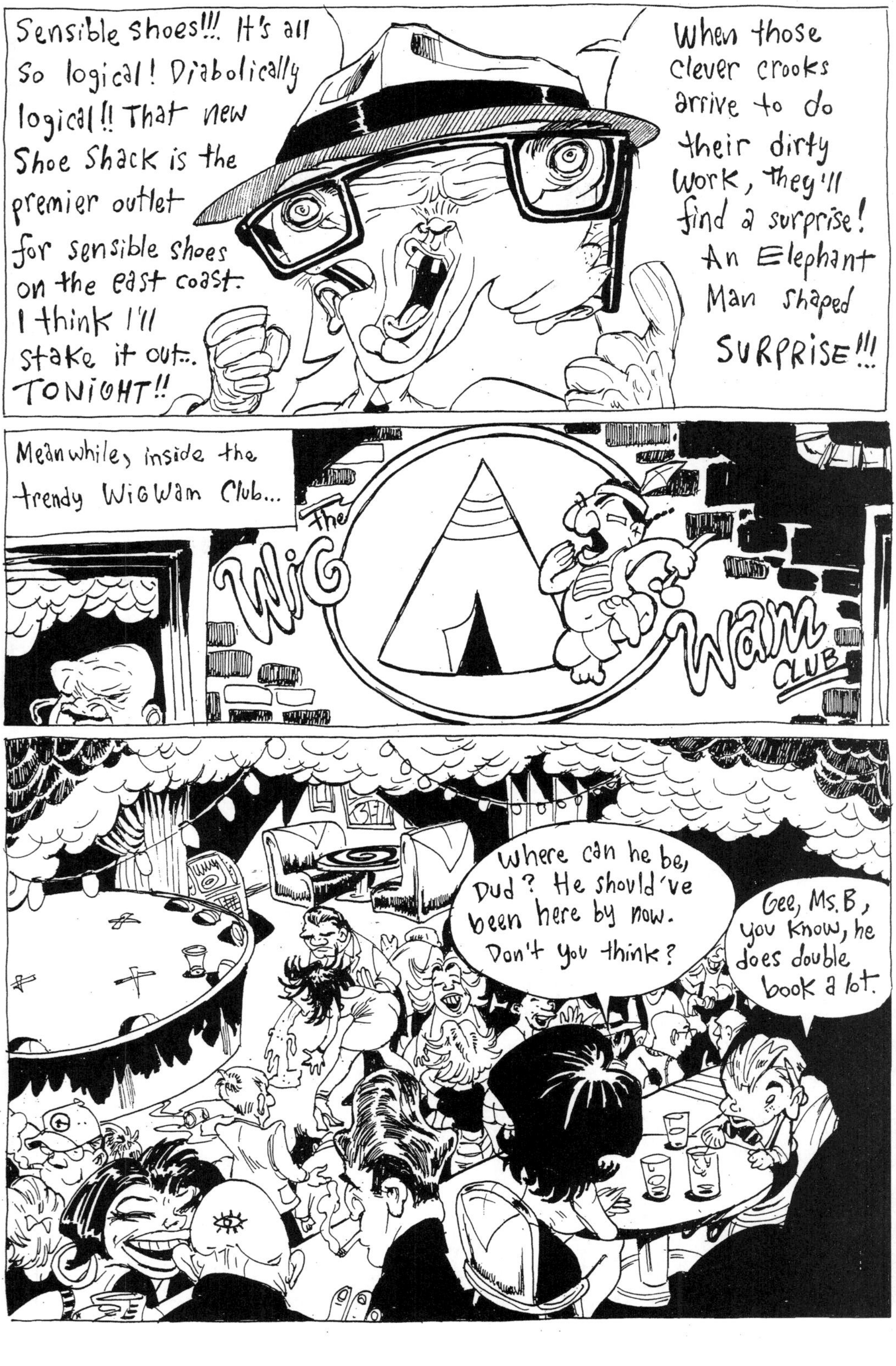

Sensible shoes!!! It's all so logical! Diabolically logical!! That new Shoe Shack is the premier outlet for sensible shoes on the east coast. I think I'll stake it out... TONIGHT!!
When those clever crooks arrive to do their dirty work, they'll find a surprise! An Elephant Man shaped SURPRISE!!!
Meanwhile, inside the trendy WigWam Club...
The Wig Wam Club
Where can he be, Dud? He should've been here by now. Don't you think?
Gee, Ms. B, you know, he does double book a lot.

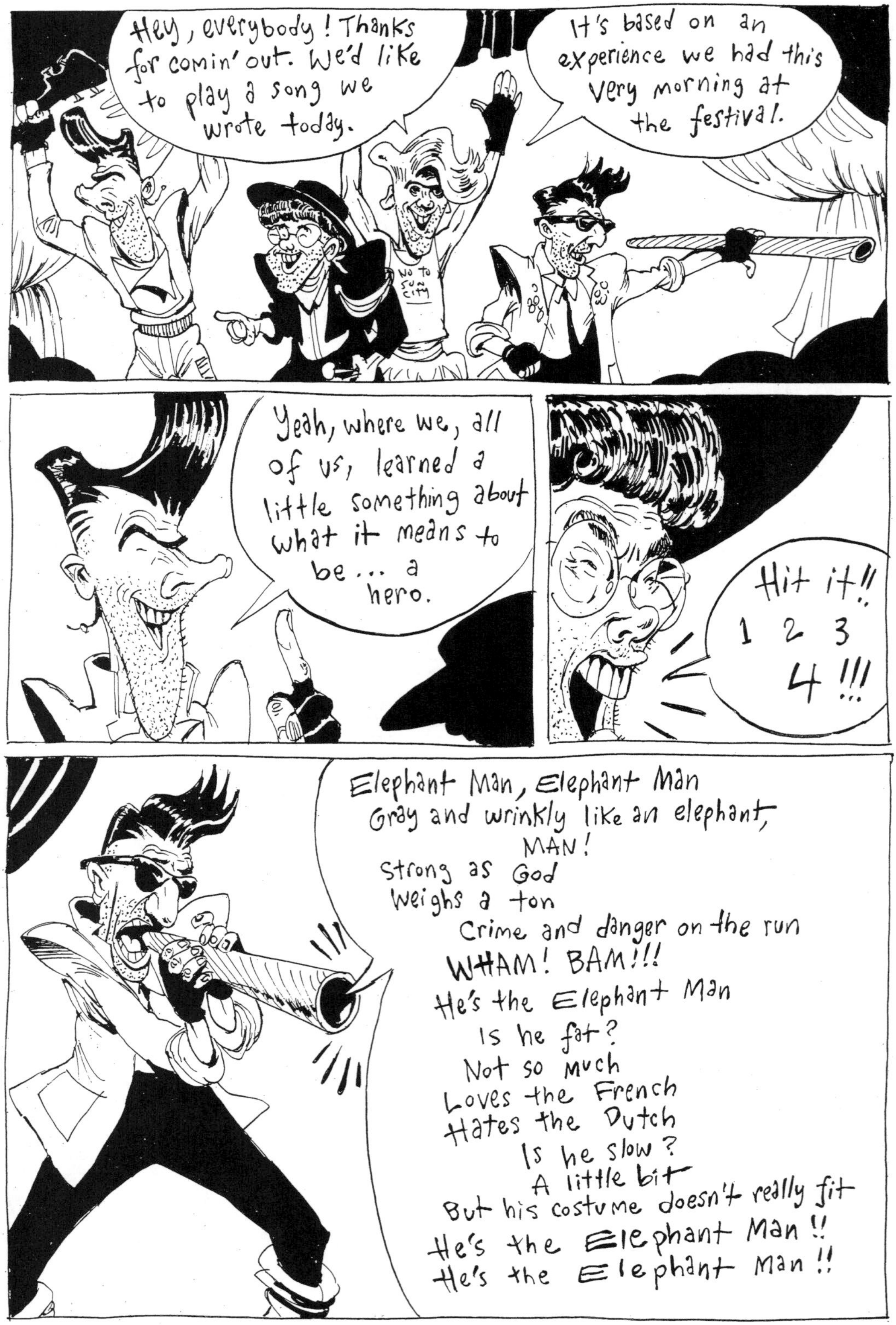
Hey, everybody! Thanks for comin' out. We'd like to play a song we wrote today.
It's based on an experience we had this very morning at the festival.
NO TO SUN CITY
Yeah, where we, all of us, learned a little something about what it means to be... a hero.
Hit it!! 1 2 3 4!!!
Elephant Man, Elephant Man
Gray and wrinkly like an elephant, MAN!
Strong as God
Weighs a ton
Crime and danger on the run
WHAM! BAM!!!
He's the Elephant Man
Is he fat?
Not so much
Loves the French
Hates the Dutch
Is he slow?
A little bit
But his costume doesn't really fit
He's the Elephant Man!!
He's the Elephant Man!!

RINGGGG
Hello? Hey, we were just talking about you.
Dud's here.
We ordered you a pink-eyed school girl with extra ice and an umbrella.
Oh? Uh huh. Well... I guess. Allright. We'll see you at work tomorrow then. Bye.
He's not coming?
He said he's got a chia pet "Situation."
Wow!
12 AM. Inside the Shoe Shack ...
SHOE SHACK
Elephant Man waits in the dark. Your time has come crooks!!!

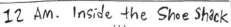

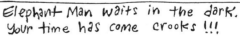

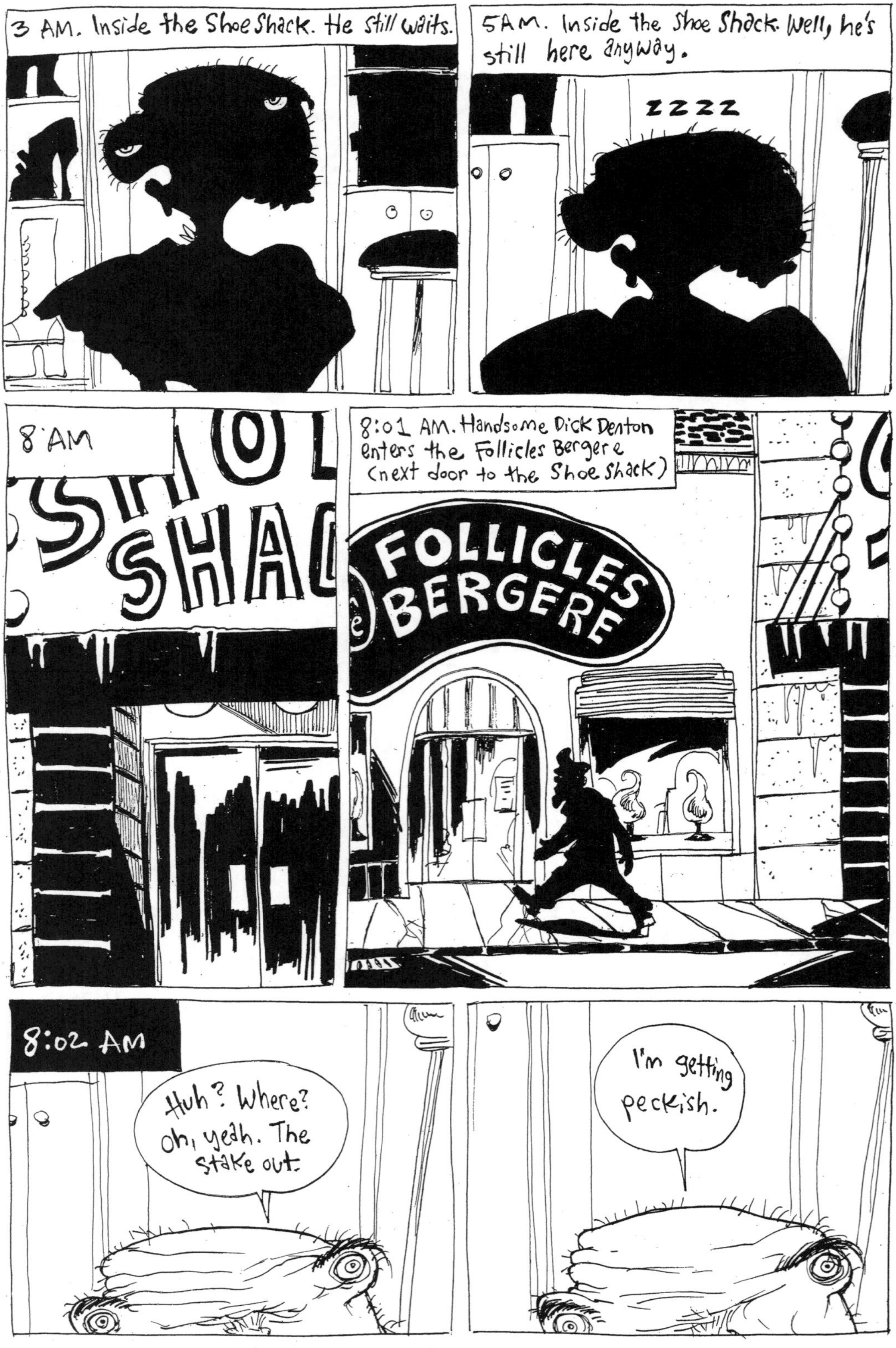
3 AM. Inside the Shoe Shack. He still waits.
5AM. Inside the Shoe Shack. Well, he's still here anyway.
ZZZZ
8 AM
SHAC
8:01 AM. Handsome Dick Denton enters the Follicles Bergere (next door to the Shoe Shack)
FOLLICLES BERGERE
8:02 AM
Huh? Where? Oh, yeah. The stake out.
I'm getting peckish.

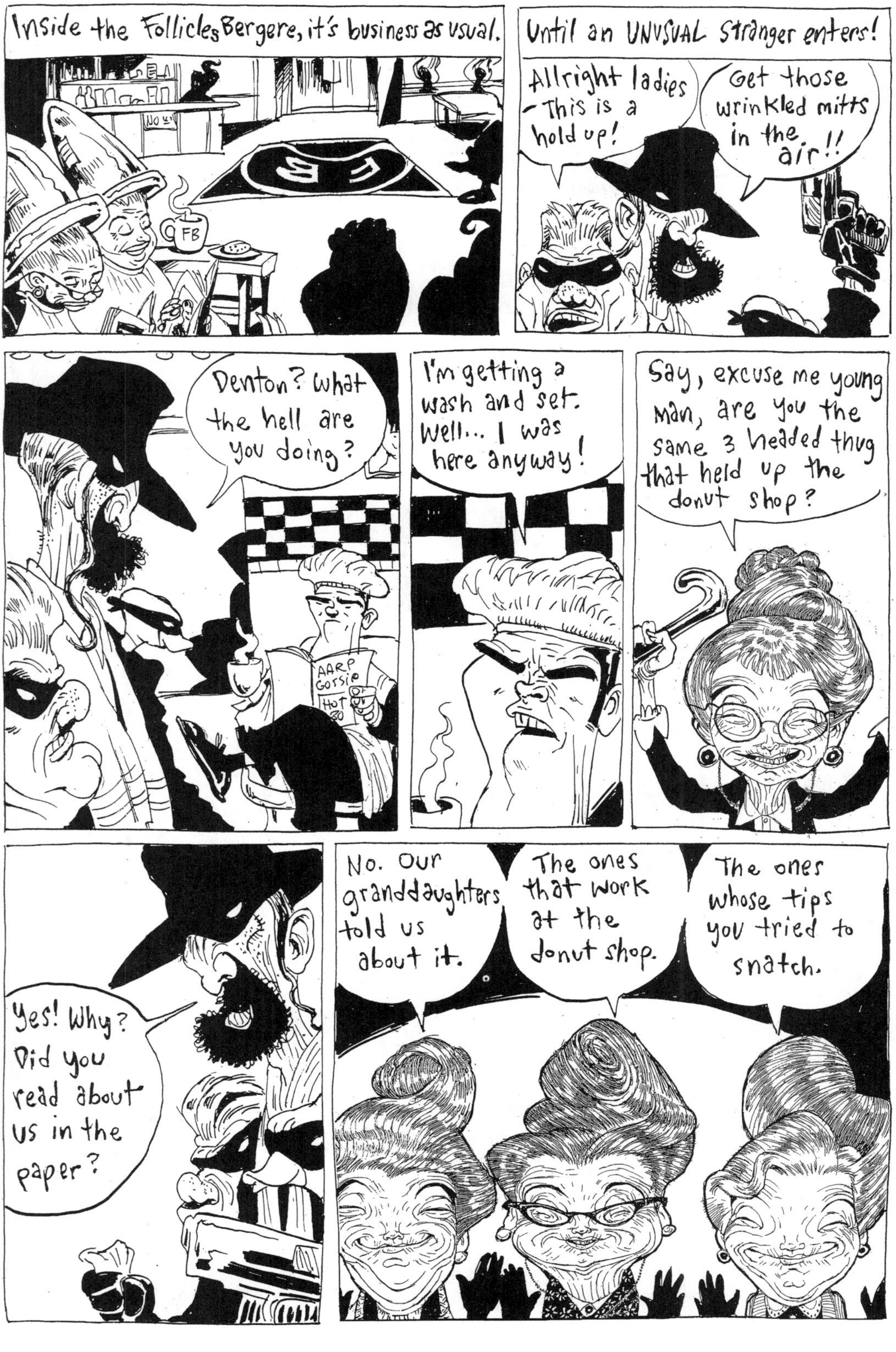
Inside the Follicles Bergere, it's business as usual.
NO
FB
FB
Until an UNUSUAL stranger enters!
Allright ladies - This is a hold up!
Get those wrinkled mitts in the air!!
Denton? What the hell are you doing?
AARP GOSSIP HOT
I'm getting a wash and set. Well... I was here anyway!
Say, excuse me young man, are you the same 3 headed thug that held up the donut shop?
Yes! Why? Did you read about us in the paper?
No. Our granddaughters told us about it.
The ones that work at the donut shop.
The ones whose tips you tried to snatch.

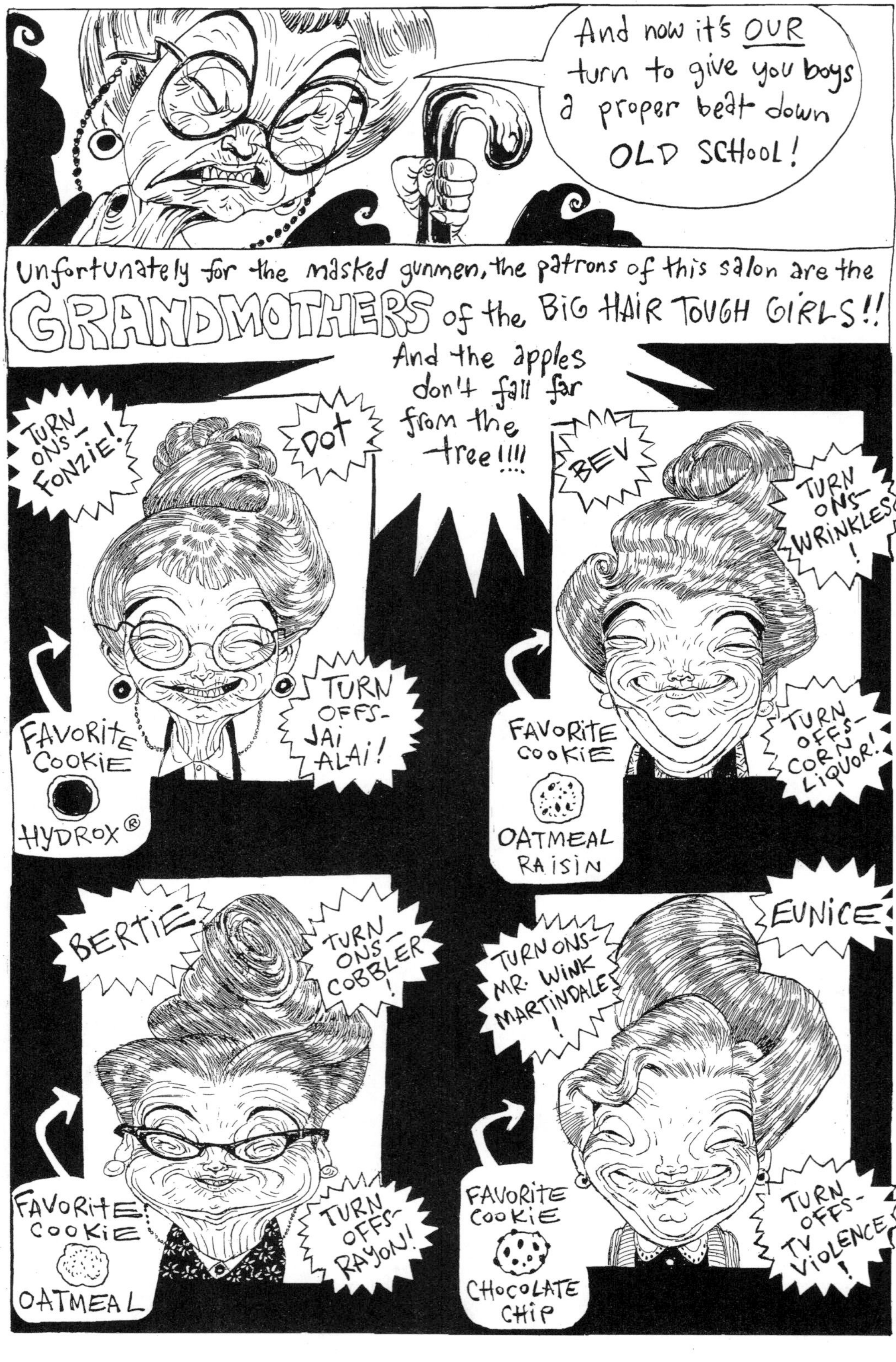
And now it's OUR turn to give you boys a proper beat down OLD SCHOOL!
Unfortunately for the masked gunmen, the patrons of this salon are the GRANDMOTHERS of the BIG HAIR TOUGH GIRLS!!
And the apples don't fall far from the tree!!!!
DOT
TURN ONS- FONZIE!
TURN OFFS- JAI ALAI!
FAVORITE COOKIE
HYDROX®
BEV
TURN ONS- WRINKLES!
TURN OFFS- CORN LIQUOR!
FAVORITE COOKIE
OATMEAL RAISIN
BERTIE
TURN ONS- COBBLER!
TURN OFFS- RAYON!
FAVORITE COOKIE
OATMEAL
EUNICE
TURN ONS- MR. WINK MARTINDALE!
TURN OFFS- TV VIOLENCE!
FAVORITE COOKIE
CHOCOLATE CHIP

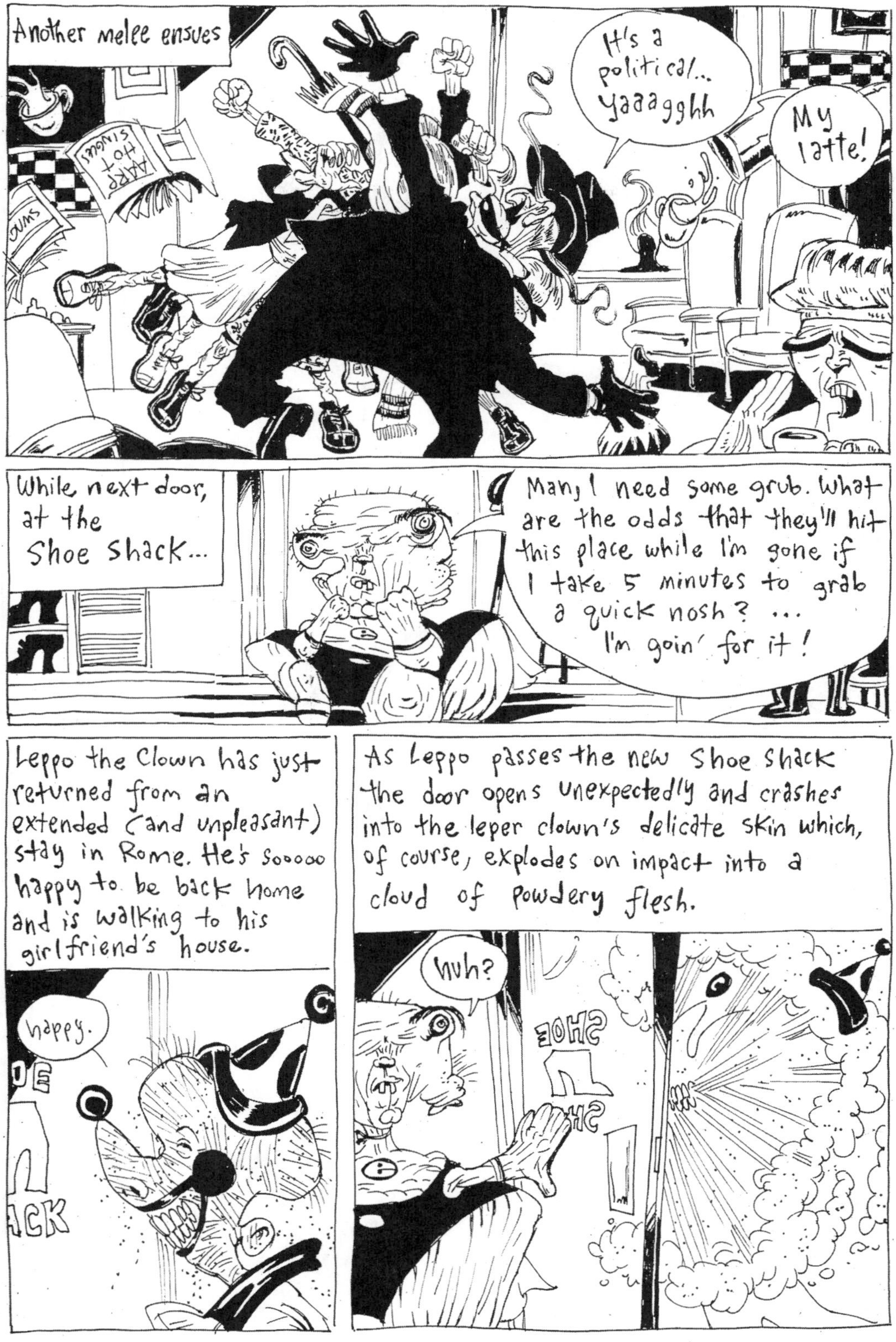

Another melee ensues
It's a political... yaaagghh
My latte!
While next door, at the Shoe Shack...
Man, I need some grub. What are the odds that they'll hit this place while I'm gone if I take 5 minutes to grab a quick nosh? ... I'm goin' for it!
Leppo the Clown has just returned from an extended (and unpleasant) stay in Rome. He's sooooo happy to be back home and is walking to his girlfriend's house.
happy.
As Leppo passes the new Shoe Shack the door opens unexpectedly and crashes into the leper clown's delicate skin which, of course, explodes on impact into a cloud of powdery flesh.
huh?

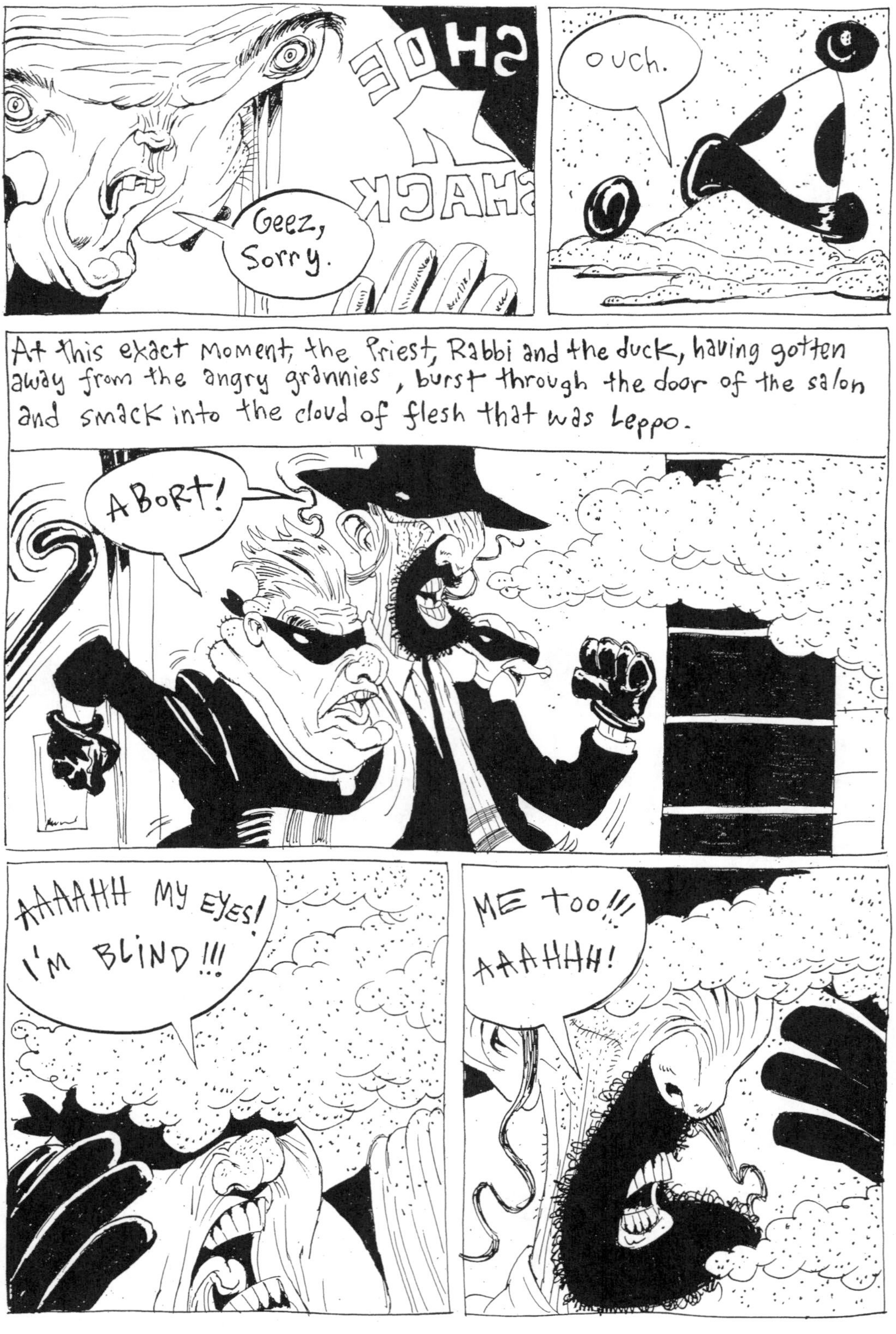

SHOE N SHACK
Geez, Sorry.
ouch.
At this exact moment, the Priest, Rabbi and the duck, having gotten away from the angry grannies, burst through the door of the salon and smack into the cloud of flesh that was Leppo.
ABORT!
AAAAHH MY EYES! I'M BLIND!!!
ME TOO!!! AAAHHH!

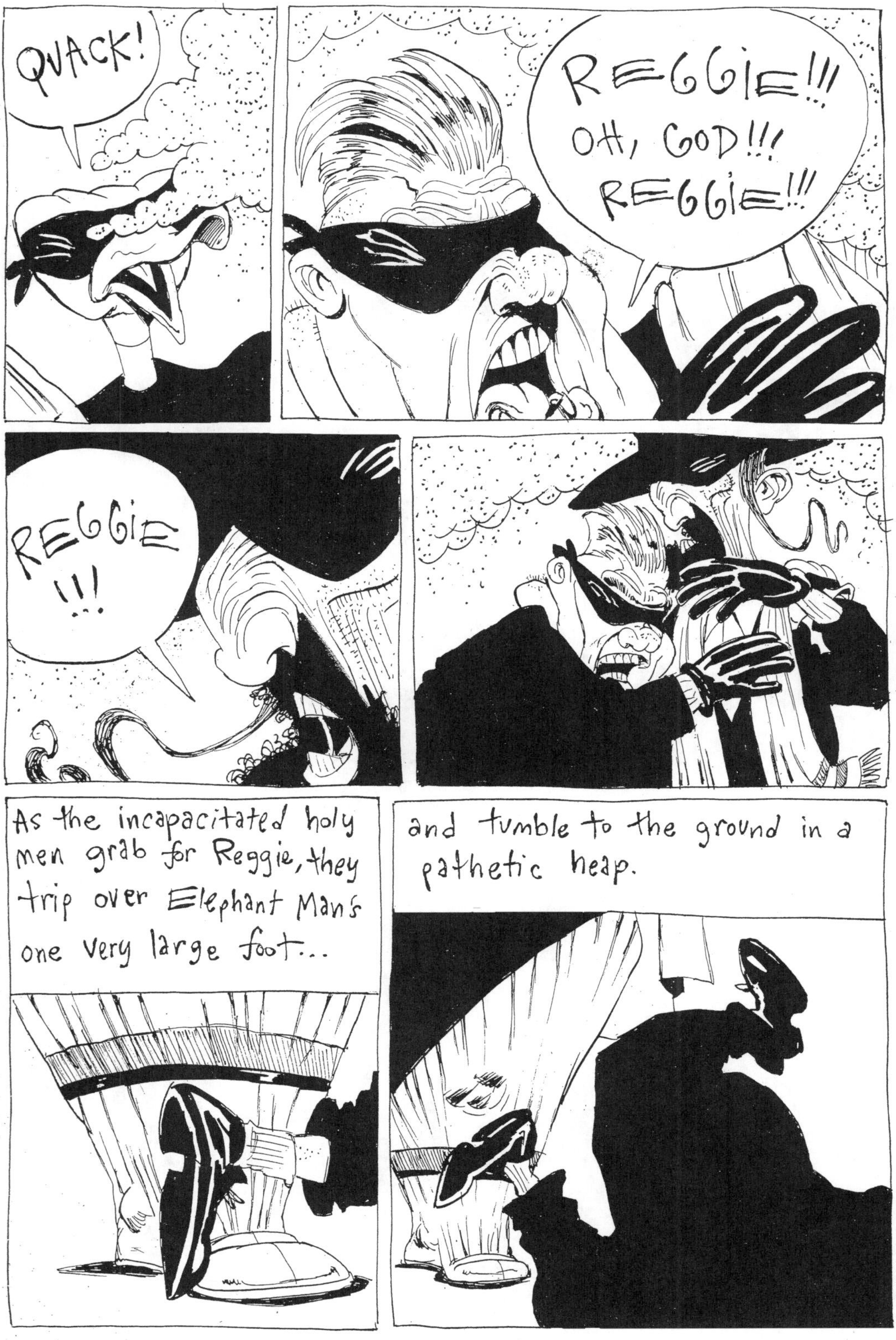
QUACK!
REGGIE!!! OH, GOD!!! REGGIE!!!
REGGIE !!!
As the incapacitated holy men grab for Reggie, they trip over Elephant Man's one very large foot...
and tumble to the ground in a pathetic heap.

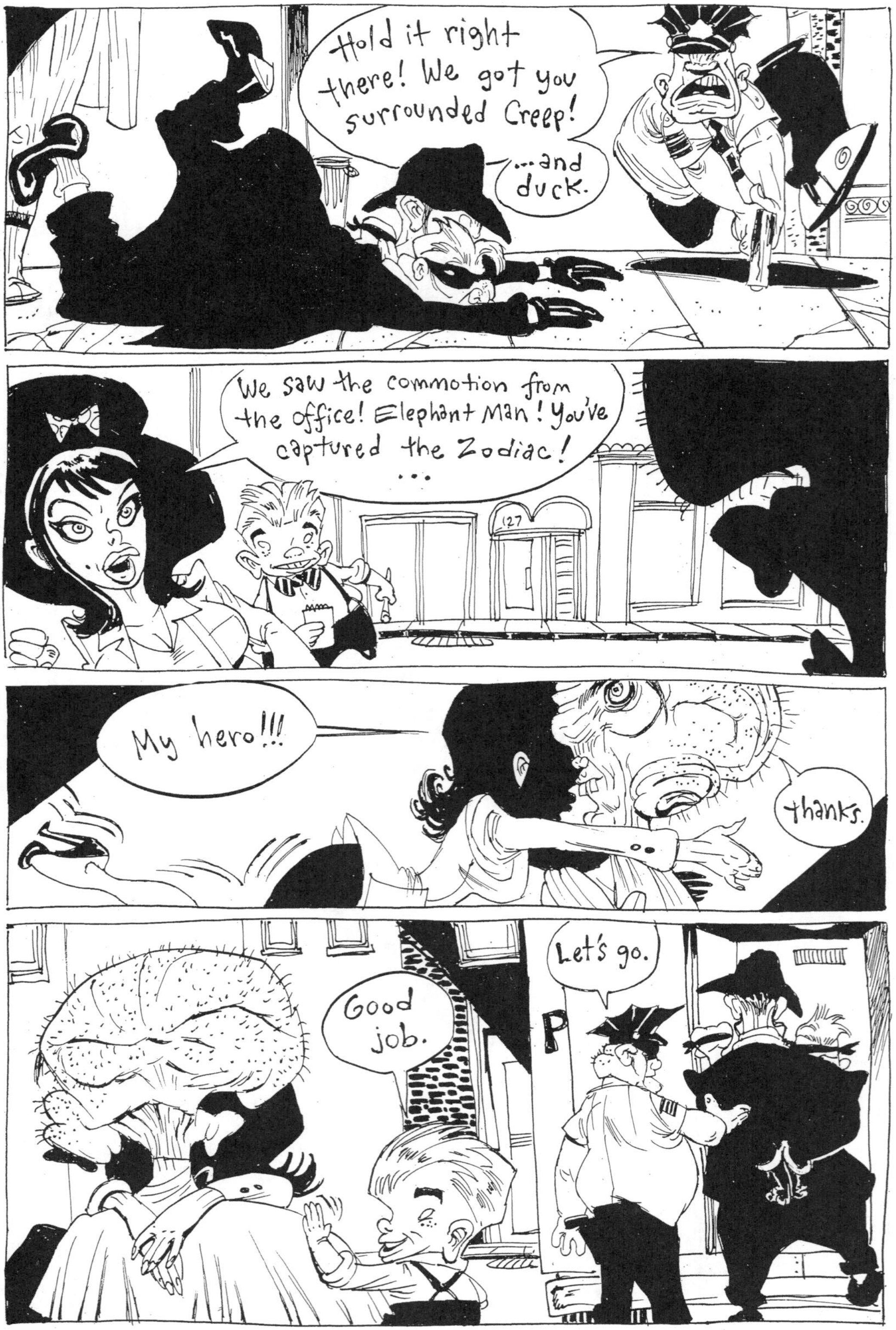
Hold it right there! We got you surrounded Creep!
...and duck.
We saw the commotion from the office! Elephant Man! You've captured the Zodiac! ...
My hero!!!
thanks.
Good job.
Let's go.

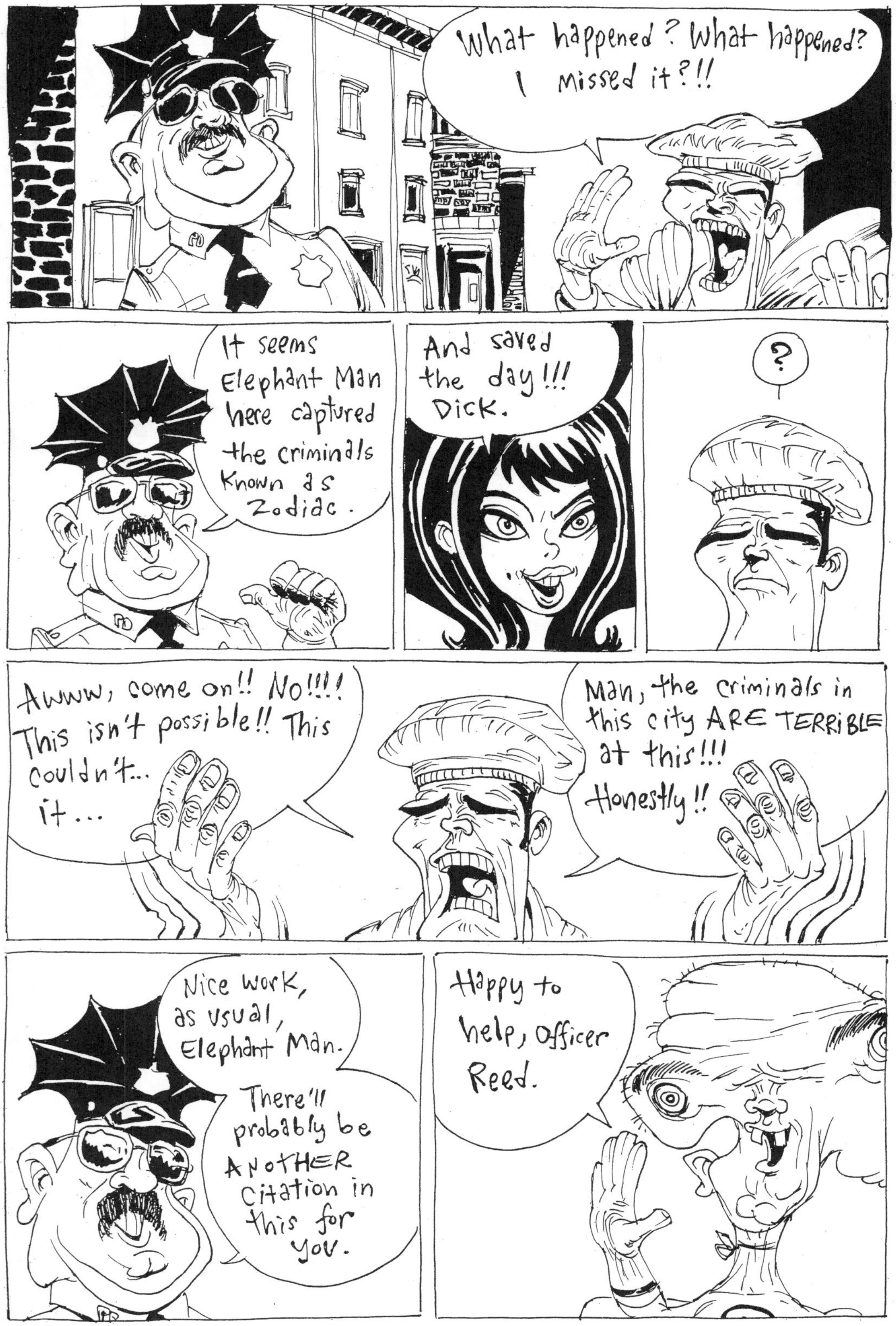

What happened? What happened? I missed it?!!
It seems Elephant Man here captured the criminals known as Zodiac.
And saved the day!!! Dick.
?
Awww, come on!! No!!!! This isn't possible!! This couldn't... it...
Man, the criminals in this city ARE TERRIBLE at this!!! Honestly!!
Nice work, as usual, Elephant Man.
There'll probably be ANOTHER citation in this for you.
Happy to help, Officer Reed.

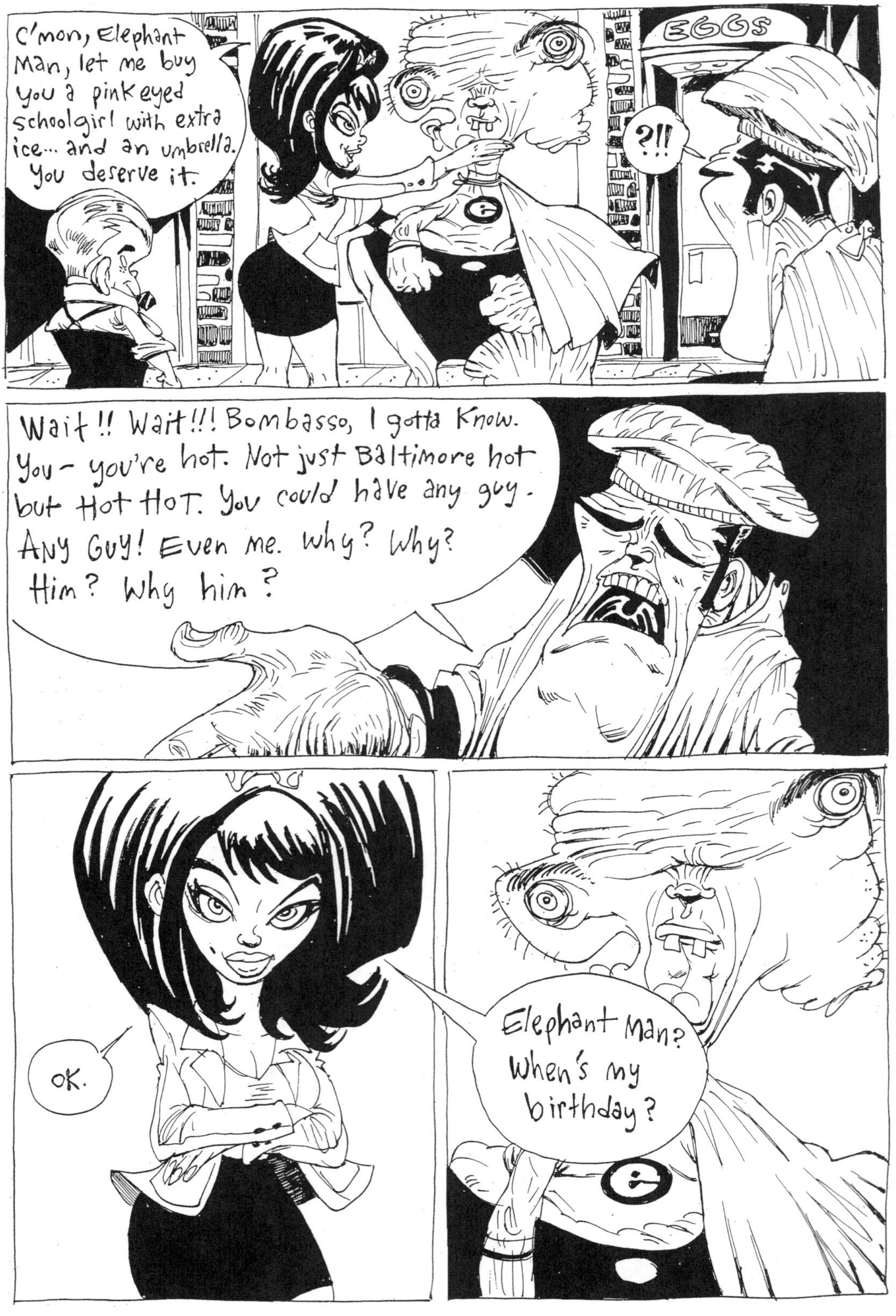
C'mon, Elephant Man, let me buy you a pinkeyed schoolgirl with extra ice... and an umbrella. You deserve it.
EGGS
?!!
Wait!! Wait!!! Bombasso, I gotta know. You - you're hot. Not just Baltimore hot but Hot HOT. You could have any guy. ANY GUY! Even me. Why? Why? Him? Why him?
OK.
Elephant Man? When's my birthday?

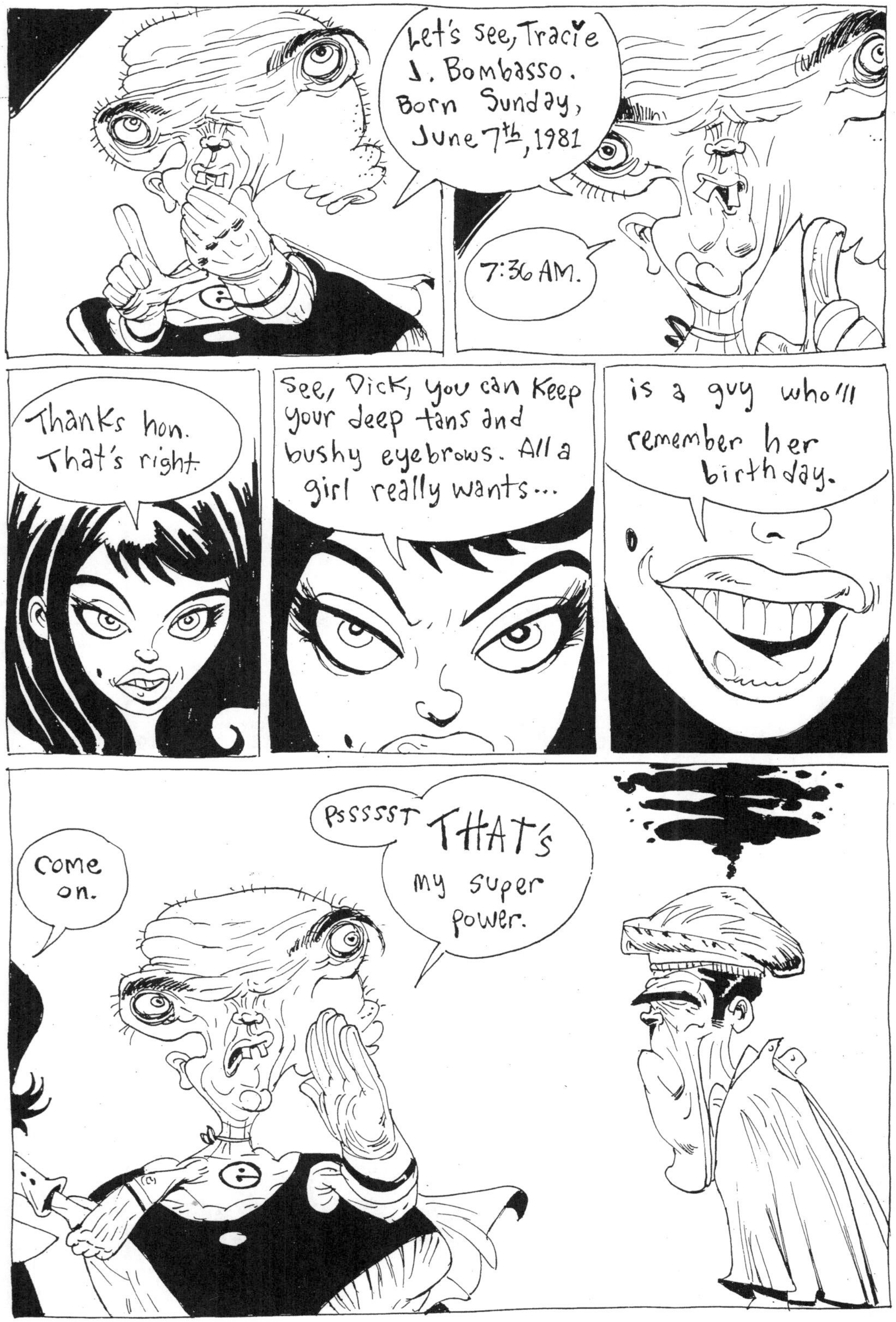

Let's see, Tracie J. Bombasso. Born Sunday, June 7th, 1981
7:36 AM.
Thanks hon. That's right.
See, Dick, you can keep your deep tans and bushy eyebrows. All a girl really wants...
is a guy who'll remember her birthday.
Come on.
PSSSSST THAT's my super power.

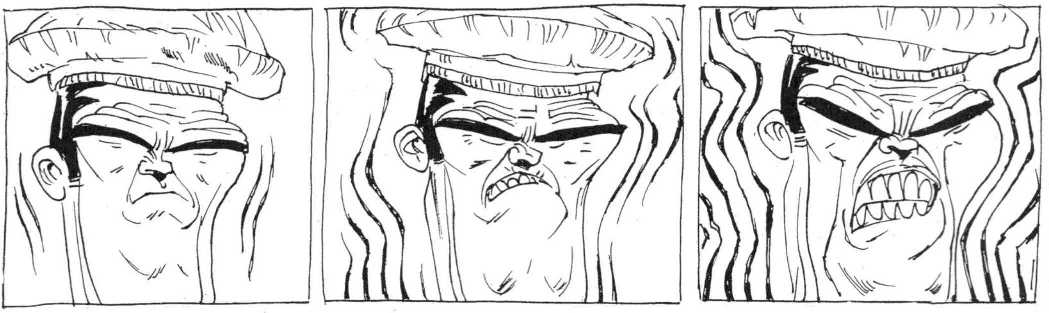

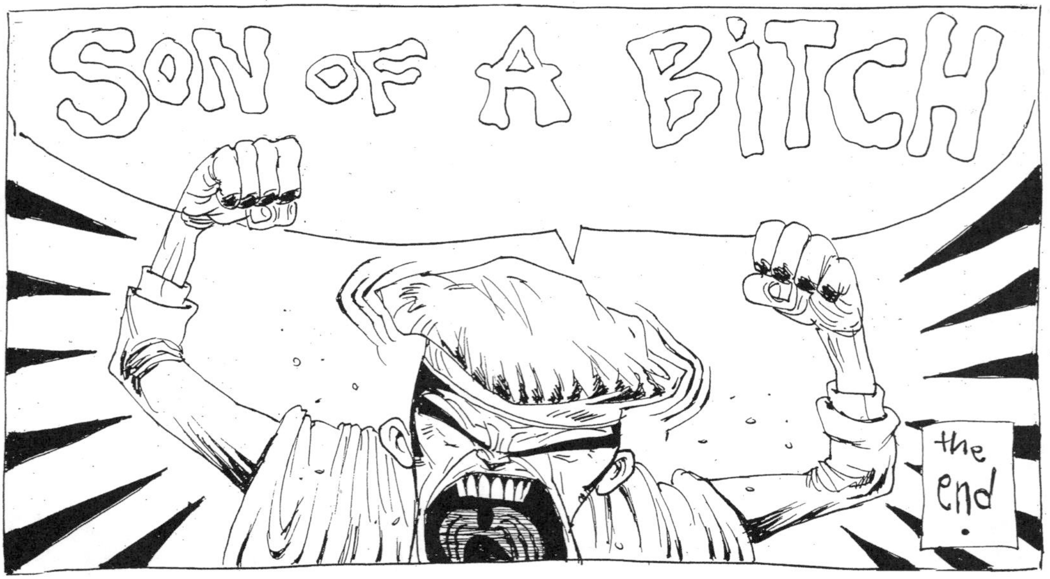
SON OF A BITCH
the end.

Next Week in Elephant Man! One of these beloved characters will... DIE!!!! Who will it be?!!!!

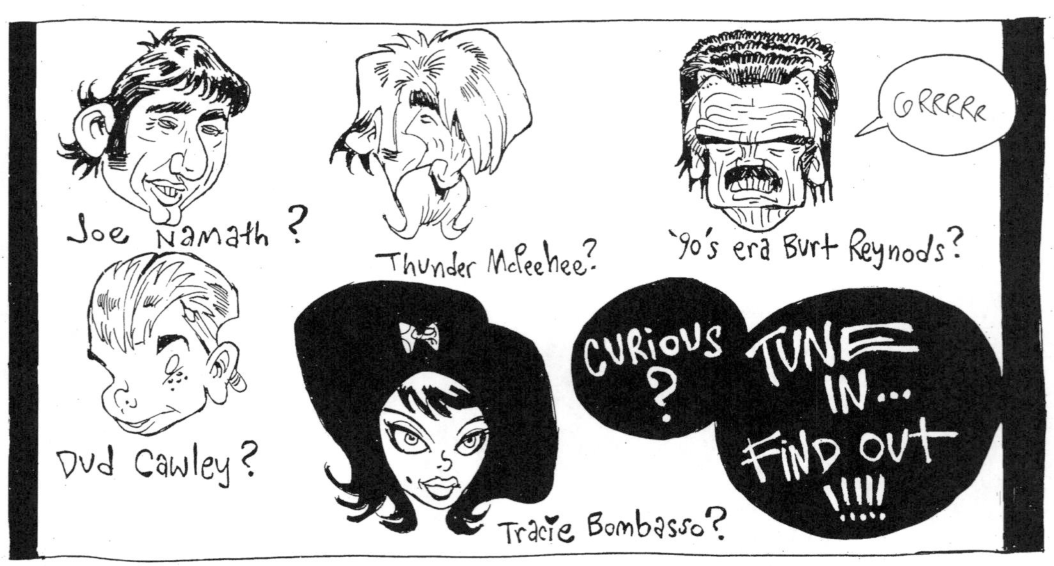
GRRRRR
Joe Namath ?
Thunder Mcleehee?
'90's era Burt Reynods?
Dud Cawley ?
CURIOUS ?
TUNE IN... FIND OUT !!!!!
Tracie Bombasso?